AFTERMATH

Princeton University Press

Princeton and Oxford

Violence

and the

Remaking

of a Self

Susan J. Brison

AFTERMATH

SUSAN J. BRISON

Earlier versions of material from chapters 1 through 4 originally appeared in
the following articles: "Surviving Sexual Violence: A Philosophical
Perspective," *Journal of Social Philosophy* 24, no. 1 (Spring 1993): 5–22; "On
the Personal as Philosophical," *American Philosophical Association Newsletter
on Feminism and Philosophy* 95, no. 1 (1995): 37–40; "Outliving Oneself:
Trauma, Memory and Personal Identity," *Feminists Rethink the Self,* ed. Diana
T. Meyers (Boulder, Colo.: Westview, 1997), 13–39; "Trauma Narratives and
the Remaking of the Self," in *Acts of Memory,* ed. Mieke Bal, Jonathan Crewe,
and Leo Spitzer (Hanover, N.H.: University Press of New England, 1999), 39–
54; "The Uses of Narrative in the Aftermath of Violence," in *On Feminist
Ethics and Politics,* ed. Claudia Card (Lawrence: University Press of Kansas,
1999), 210–225.

Library of Congress Cataloging-in-Publication Data

Brison, Susan J.

    Aftermath: violence and the remaking of a self / Susan J. Brison.

      p. cm.

    Includes bibliographical references and index.

    ISBN 0-691-01619-4

    1. Rape victims—Psychology.   2. Victims of violent crimes—
Psychology.   3. Traumatic shock.   I. Title.

    HV6558 .B75 2001

    362.88—dc21   2001021268

British Library Cataloging-in Publication Data is available

This book has been composed in Minion.

Printed on acid-free paper. ∞

www.pup.princeton.edu

Printed in the United States of America

10 9 8 7 6 5 4 3 2 1

For Gabriel,

who arrived,

and Tom,

who stayed

Contents

af·ter·math, n. 1. Something that results or follows from
an event, esp. one of a disastrous or unfortunate
nature. . . . . 2. a new growth of grass following one or
more mowings.[1]

Preface

Ten years ago, a few months after I had survived a nearly
fatal sexual assault and attempted murder in the south of
France, I sat down at my computer to write about it for the
first time and all I could come up with was a list of paradoxes. Things had stopped making sense. I thought it was
quite possible that I was brain-damaged as a result of the
head injuries I had sustained. Or perhaps the heightened
lucidity I had experienced during the assault remained, giving me a clearer, although profoundly disorienting, picture
of the world. I turned to philosophy for meaning and consolation and could find neither. Had my reasoning broken
down? Or was it the breakdown of reason? I couldn't explain
what had happened to me. I was attacked for no reason. I
had ventured outside the human community, landed beyond

the moral universe, beyond the realm of predictable events and comprehensible actions, and I didn't know how to get back.

As a philosopher, I was used to taking something apparently obvious and familiar—the nature of time, say, or the relation between words and things—and making it into something quite puzzling and strange. But now, when I was confronted with the utterly strange and paradoxical, philosophy was of no use in making me feel at home in the world.

After I was rescued and taken to the Grenoble hospital, I was told repeatedly how "lucky" I was to be alive, and for a short while I even believed this myself. At the time I did not yet know how trauma not only haunts the conscious and unconscious mind, but also remains in the body, in each of the senses, ready to resurface whenever something triggers a reliving of the traumatic event. I didn't know that the worst—the unimaginably painful aftermath of violence—was yet to come.

One of the most difficult aspects of my recovery from the assault was the seeming inability of others to remember what had happened, accompanied by their habit of exhorting me, too, to forget. Although I was initially surprised by this response, once I discovered how typical it was, I became more aware of the intense psychological pressures that make it difficult for all of us to empathize with victims of trauma. The prevalent lack of empathy with trauma victims, which is reinforced by the cultural repression of memories of violence and victimization (for example, in the United States about slavery, in Germany and Poland and elsewhere about the Holocaust), results, I realized, not merely from ignorance or indifference, but also from an active fear of identifying with those whose terrifying fate forces us to acknowledge that we are not in control of our own.

Nonetheless, the trauma survivor must find empathic listeners in order to carry on. Piecing together a shattered self requires a process of remembering and working through in which speech and affect converge in a trauma narrative. In this book I explore the performative aspect of speech in testimonies of trauma: how *saying* something about the memory *does* something to it. The communicative act of bearing witness to traumatic events not only transforms traumatic memories into narratives that can then be integrated into the survivor's sense of self and view of the world, but it also reintegrates the survivor into a community, re-establishing bonds of trust and faith in others.

The challenge of finding language that is true to traumatic experience is, however, a daunting one. How can we speak about the unspeakable without attempting to render it intelligible and sayable? The paradoxes of traumatic memory may seem to defy analysis. Our ordinary concepts of time and identity cease to apply, as in the French writer Charlotte Delbo's statement, "I died in Auschwitz, but no one knows it" (1995, 267). For months after my assault, I had to stop myself before saying (what seemed accurate at the time), "I was murdered in France last summer." In this book, I attempt to explain these cryptic observations, and, in so doing, I develop and defend a view of the self as fundamentally relational—capable of being undone by violence, but also of being remade in connection with others.

Since I have found that writing about trauma challenges not only accepted views of the limits of language and logic, but also current assumptions about appropriate scholarly methodology, I have employed a range of what I consider to be complementary methodologies: my own process of "working through," cultural analysis, feminist criticism, philosophical theorizing about the self, and an examination of clinical and neurological studies of trauma. The result is a record of my thinking about trauma and recovery over the past ten years. The chronology of this period, however, is fractured in the telling. Time may be linear (who knows?) but the aftermath was not. There have been many periods of progress and of decline, victories and setbacks, both major and minor. I have changed during this time and so have my views, but, rather than revise my earlier writings in light of more recent understandings, I have tried to convey the trajectory of my ideas. As Ursula Le Guin writes, "It doesn't seem right or wise to revise an old text severely, as if trying to obliterate it, hiding the evidence that one had to go there to get here. It is rather in the feminist mode to let one's changes of mind, and the processes of change, stand as evidence."[2]

Interwoven with a philosophical examination of violence and its aftermath is a first-person narrative of remaking a self shattered by trauma. Chapter 1, an account of philosophical issues raised by my assault and the immediate aftermath, was written during the two years after my assault. It is an examination of the way trauma shatters one's most fundamental assumptions about the world, including beliefs about our ability to control what happens to us. This chapter would be different in many ways were I to write it now—less angry, less urgent, and somewhat more detached. But I have left it in its original form (except for a few minor stylistic revisions) in order to convey my perspective soon after the event. Chapter 2 is a development and defense of the methodology used throughout the book. In it I argue for the necessity of first-person narratives in facilitating our understanding of trauma and victimization. In chapters 3 and 4 I discuss the therapeutic function of trauma narratives and, in chapter 5, I examine their role in constructing and changing cultural tropes and political norms. In chapter 6, I explore the tensions among the various functions of narrative, in particular, the tension between living to tell and telling to live, that is, between getting (and keeping) the story right in order to bear witness and being able to rewrite the story in ways that enable the survivor to go on with her life.

My assailant was apprehended, convicted of rape and attempted murder, and sentenced to ten years in prison. His sentence is finished today. It's tempting to think, as I release this book into the world, that mine is, too, although I know there will be many returns of the day, more occasions for telling and retelling the story. But right now, as I look out at the freshly mown field behind our house in Vermont, all I see and hear is new life—shoots of grass, lupines, pine trees, fireflies, crickets, frogs, small things singing. And I'm surrounded by the warmth and sweetness of friends and family and music. We may call such things reasons to live, but reason has little to do with it. They are the embodiments of our wishes and passions, the hopes and desires that draw us into the future.

Thetford, Vermont
Independence Day
July 2000

Surviving Sexual Violence

C H A P T E R   O N E

On July 4, 1990, at 10:30 in the morning, I went for a walk along a peaceful-looking country road in a village outside Grenoble, France. It was a gorgeous day, and I didn't envy my husband, Tom, who had to stay inside and work on a manuscript with a French colleague of his. I sang to myself as I set out, stopping to pet a goat and pick a few wild strawberries along the way. About an hour and a half later, I was lying face down in a muddy creek bed at the bottom of a dark ravine, struggling to stay alive. I had been grabbed from behind, pulled into the bushes, beaten, and sexually assaulted. Feeling absolutely helpless and entirely at my assailant's mercy, I talked to him, calling him "sir." I tried to appeal to his humanity, and, when that failed, I addressed myself to his self-interest. He called me a whore and told me to shut up.

Although I had said I'd do whatever he wanted, as the sexual assault began I instinctively fought back, which so enraged my attacker that he strangled me until I lost consciousness. When I awoke, I was being dragged by my feet down into the ravine. I had often, while dreaming, thought I was awake, but now I was awake and convinced I was having a nightmare. But it was no dream. After ordering me, in a gruff, Gestapo-like voice, to get on my hands and knees, my assailant strangled me again. I wish I could convey the horror of losing consciousness while my animal instincts desperately fought the effects of strangulation. This time I was sure I was dying. But I revived, just in time to see him lunging toward me with a rock. He smashed it into my forehead, knocking me out, and eventually, after another strangulation attempt, he left me for dead.

After my assailant left, I managed to climb out of the ravine, and was rescued by a farmer, who called the police, a doctor, and an ambulance. I was taken to emergency at the Grenoble hospital where I underwent neurological tests, x-rays, blood tests, and a gynecological exam. Leaves and twigs were taken from my hair for evidence, my fingernails were scraped, and my mouth was swabbed for samples. I had multiple head injuries, my eyes were swollen shut, and I had a fractured trachea, which made breathing difficult. I was not permitted to drink or eat anything for the first thirty hours, although Tom, who never left my side, was allowed to dab my blood-encrusted lips with a wet towel. The next day, I was transferred out of emergency and into my own room. But I could not be left alone, even for a few minutes. I was terrified my assailant would find me and finish the job. When someone later brought in the local paper with a story about my attack, I was greatly relieved that it referred to me as *Mlle M. R.* and didn't mention that I was an American. Even by the time I left the hospital, eleven days later, I was so concerned about my assailant tracking me down that I put only my lawyer's address on the hospital records.

Although fears for my safety may have initially explained why I wanted to remain anonymous, by that time my assailant had been apprehended, indicted for rape and attempted murder, and incarcerated without possibility of bail. Still, I didn't want people to know that I had been sexually assaulted. I don't know whether this was because I could still hardly believe it myself, because keeping this information confidential was one of the few ways I could feel in control of my life, or because, in spite of my conviction that I had done nothing wrong, I felt ashamed.

When I started telling people about the attack, I said, simply, that I was the victim of an attempted murder. People typically asked, in horror, "What was the motivation? Were you mugged?" and when I replied, "No, it started as a sexual assault," most inquirers were satisfied with that as an explanation of why some man wanted to murder me. I would have thought that a murder attempt plus a sexual assault would require more, not less, of an explanation than a murder attempt by itself. (After all, there are two criminal acts to explain here.)

One reason sexual violence is taken for granted by many is because it is so very prevalent. The FBI, notorious for underestimating the frequency of sex crimes, notes that, in the United States, a rape occurs on an average of every six minutes.[1] But this figure covers only the reported cases of rape, and some researchers claim that only about 10 percent of all rapes get reported.[2] Every fifteen seconds, a woman is beaten.[3] The everydayness of sexual violence, as evidenced by these mind-numbing statistics, leads many to think that male violence against women is natural, a given, something not in need of explanation and not amenable to change. And yet, through some extraordinary mental gymnastics, while most people take sexual violence for granted, they simultaneously manage to deny that it really exists—or, rather, that it could happen to them. We continue to think that we—and the women we love—are immune to it, provided, that is, that we don't do anything "foolish." How many of us have swallowed the potentially lethal lie that if you don't do anything wrong, if you're just careful enough, you'll be safe? How many of us have believed its damaging, victim-blaming corollary: if you are attacked, it's because you did something wrong? These are lies, and in telling my story I hope to expose them, as well as to help bridge the gap between those who have been victimized and those who have not.

Sexual violence and its aftermath raise numerous philosophical issues in a variety of areas in our discipline. The disintegration of the self experienced by victims of violence challenges our notions of personal identity over time, a major preoccupation of metaphysics. A victim's seemingly justified skepticism about everyone and everything is pertinent to epistemology, especially if the goal of epistemology is, as Wilfrid Sellars put it, that of feeling at home in the world. In aesthetics, as well as in philosophy of law, the discussion of sexual violence in- or as- art could use the illumination provided by a victim's perspective. Perhaps the most important issues posed by sexual violence are in the areas of social, political, and legal philosophy, and insight into these, as well, requires an understanding of what it's like to be a victim of such violence.

One of the very few articles written by philosophers on violence against women is Ross Harrison's "Rape: A Case

Study in Political Philosophy."[4] In this article Harrison argues that not only do utilitarians need to assess the harmfulness of rape in order to decide whether the harm to the victim outweighs the benefit to the rapist, but even on a rights-based approach to criminal justice we need to be able to assess the benefits and harms involved in criminalizing and punishing violent acts such as rape. In his view, it is not always the case, contra Ronald Dworkin, that rights trump considerations of utility, so, even on a rights-based account of justice, we need to give an account of why, in the case of rape, the pleasure gained by the perpetrator (or by multiple perpetrators, in the case of gang-rape) is always outweighed by the harm done to the victim. He points out the peculiar difficulty most of us have in imagining the pleasure a rapist gets out of an assault, but, he asserts confidently, "There is no problem imagining what it is like to be a victim" (Harrison 1986, 51). To his credit, he acknowledges the importance, to political philosophy, of trying to imagine others' experience, for otherwise we could not compare harms and benefits, which he argues must be done even in cases of conflicts of rights in order to decide which of competing rights should take priority. But imagining what it is like to be a rape victim is no simple matter, since much of what a victim goes through is unimaginable. Still, it's essential to try to convey it.

In my efforts to tell the victim's story—my story, our story—I've been inspired and instructed not only by feminist philosophers who have refused to accept the dichotomy between the personal and the political, but also by critical race theorists such as Patricia Williams, Mari Matsuda, and Charles Lawrence, who have incorporated first-person narrative accounts into their discussions of the law. In writing about hate speech, they have argued persuasively that one cannot do justice to the issues involved in debates about restrictions on speech without listening to the victims' stories.[5] In describing the effects of racial harassment on victims, they have departed from the academic convention of speaking in the impersonal, "universal," voice and relate incidents they themselves experienced. In her groundbreaking book, *The Alchemy of Race and Rights* (1991), Williams describes how it felt to learn about her great-great-grandmother, who was purchased at age 11 by a slave owner who raped and impregnated her the following year. And in describing instances of everyday racism she herself has lived through, she gives us imaginative access to what it's like to be the victim of racial discrimination. Some may consider such first-person accounts in academic writing to be self-indulgent, but I consider them a welcome antidote to scholarship that, in the guise of universality, tends to silence those who most need to be heard.

Philosophers are far behind legal theorists in acknowledging the need for a diversity of voices. We are trained to write in an abstract, universal voice and to shun first-person narratives as biased and inappropriate for academic discourse. Some topics, however, such as the impact of racial and sexual violence on victims, cannot even be broached unless those affected by such crimes can tell of their experiences in their own words. Unwittingly further illustrating the need for the victim's perspective, Harrison writes, elsewhere in his article on rape, "What principally distinguishes rape from normal sexual activity is the consent of the raped woman" (Harrison 1986, 52). There is no parallel to this in the case of other crimes, such as theft or murder. Try "What principally distinguishes theft from normal gift-giving is the consent of the person stolen from." We don't think of theft as "coerced gift-giving." We don't think of murder as "assisted suicide minus consent." Why not? In the latter case, it could be because assisted suicide is relatively rare (even compared with murder) and so it's odd to use it as the more familiar thing to which we are analogizing. But in the former case, gift-giving is presumably more prevalent than theft (at least in academic circles) and yet it still sounds odd to explicate theft in terms of gift-giving minus consent (or coerced philanthropy). In the cases of both theft and murder, the notion of violation seems built into our conceptions of the physical acts constituting the crimes, so it is inconceivable that one could consent to the act in question. Why is it so easy for a philosopher such as Harrison to think of rape, however, as "normal sexual activity minus consent"? This may be because the nature of the violation in the case of rape hasn't been all that obvious. Witness the phenomenon of rape jokes, the prevalence of pornography glorifying rape, the common attitude that, in the case of women, "no" means "yes," that women really want it.[6]

Since I was assaulted by a stranger, in a "safe" place, and was so visibly injured when I encountered the police and medical personnel, I was, throughout my hospitalization and my dealings with the police, spared the insult, suffered by so many rape victims, of not being believed or of being said to have asked for the attack. However, it became clear to me as I gave my deposition from my hospital bed that this would still be an issue in my assailant's trial. During my deposition, I recalled being on the verge of giving up my struggle to live when I was galvanized by a sudden, piercing image of Tom's future pain on finding my corpse in that ravine. At this point in my deposition, I paused, glanced over at the police officer who was typing the transcript, and asked whether it was appropriate to include this image of my husband in my recounting of the facts. The gendarme replied that it definitely was and that it was a very good thing I mentioned my husband, since my assailant, who had confessed to the sexual assault, was claiming I had provoked it. As serious as the occasion was, and as much as it hurt to laugh, I couldn't help it, the suggestion was so ludicrous. Could it have been those baggy Gap jeans I was wearing that morning? Or was it the heavy sweatshirt? My maddeningly seductive jogging shoes? Or was it simply my walking along minding my own business that had provoked his murderous rage?

After I completed my deposition, which lasted eight hours, the police officer asked me to read and sign the transcript he'd typed to certify that it was accurate. I was surprised to see that it began with the words, "*Comme je suis sportive . . .* " ("Since I am athletic . . . ")—added by the police to explain what possessed me to go for a walk by myself that fine morning. I was too exhausted by this point to protest "No, I'm not an athlete, I'm a philosophy professor," and I figured the officer knew what he was doing, so I let it stand. That evening, my assailant was formally indicted. I retained a lawyer, and met him along with the investigating magistrate, when I gave my second deposition toward the end of my hospitalization. Although what occurred was officially a crime against the state, not against me, I was advised to pursue a civil suit in order to recover unreimbursed medical expenses, and, in any case, I needed an advocate to explain the French legal system to me. I was told that since this was an "easy" case, the trial would occur within a year. In fact, the trial took place two and a half years after the assault, due to the delaying tactics of my assailant's lawyer, who was trying to get him off on an insanity defense. According to article 64 of the French criminal code, if the defendant is determined to have been insane at the time, then, legally, there was "*ni crime, ni délit*"—neither crime nor offense. The jury, however, did not accept the insanity plea and found my assailant guilty of rape and attempted murder.

As things turned out, my experience with the criminal justice system was better than that of most sexual assault victims. I did, however, occasionally get glimpses of the humiliating insensitivity victims routinely endure. Before I could be released from the hospital, for example, I had to undergo a second forensic examination at a different hospital. I was taken in a wheelchair out to a hospital van, driven to another hospital, taken to an office where there were no receptionists and where I was greeted by two male doctors I had never seen before. When they told me to take off my clothes and stand in the middle of the room, I refused. I had to ask for a hospital gown to put on. For about an hour the two of them went over me like a piece of meat, calling out measurements of bruises and other assessments of damage, as if they were performing an autopsy. This was just the first of many incidents in which I felt as if I was experiencing things posthumously. When the inconceivable happens, one starts to doubt even the most mundane, realistic perceptions. Perhaps I'm not really here, I thought, perhaps I did die in that ravine. The line between life and death, once so clear and sustaining, now seemed carelessly drawn and easily erased.

For the first several months after my attack, I led a spectral existence, not quite sure whether I had died and the world went on without me, or whether I was alive but in a totally alien world. Tom and I returned to the States, and I continued to convalesce, but I felt as though I'd somehow outlived myself. I sat in our apartment and stared outside for hours, through the blur of a detached vitreous, feeling like Robert Lowell's newly widowed mother, described in one of his poems as mooning in a window "as if she had stayed on a train / one stop past her destination."[7]

My sense of unreality was fed by the massive denial of those around me—a reaction I learned is an almost universal response to rape. Where the facts would appear to be incontrovertible, denial takes the shape of attempts to explain the assault in ways that leave the observers' worldview unscathed. Even those who are able to acknowledge the existence of violence try to protect themselves from the realization that the world in which it occurs is their world and so they find it hard to identify with the victim. They cannot allow themselves to imagine the victim's shattered life, or else their illusions about their own safety and control over their own lives might begin to crumble. The most well-meaning individuals, caught up in the myth of their own immunity, can inadvertently add to the victim's suffering by suggesting that the attack was avoidable or somehow her fault. One victims' assistance coordinator, whom I had phoned for legal advice, stressed that she herself had never been a victim and said that I would benefit from the experience by learning not to be so trusting of people and to take basic safety precautions like not going out alone late at night. She didn't pause long enough during her lecture for me to point out that I was attacked suddenly, from behind, in broad daylight.

We are not taught to empathize with victims. In crime novels and detective films, it is the villain, or the one who solves the murder mystery, who attracts our attention; the victim, a merely passive pretext for our entertainment, is conveniently disposed of—and forgotten—early on. We identify with the agents' strength and skill, for good or evil, and join the victim, if at all, only in our nightmares. Although one might say, as did Clarence Thomas, looking at convicted criminals on their way to jail, "but for the grace of God, there go I,"[8] a victim's fate prompts an almost instinctive "it could never happen to me." This may explain why there is, in our criminal justice system, so little concern for justice for victims—especially rape victims. They have no constitutionally protected rights *qua* victims. They have no right to a speedy trial or to compensation for damages (although states have been changing this in recent years), or to privacy vis-à-vis the press. As a result of their victimization, they often lose their jobs, their homes, their spouses—in addition to a great deal of money, time, sleep, self-esteem, and peace of mind. The rights to "life, liberty, and the pursuit of happiness," possessed, in the abstract, by all of us, are of little use to victims who can lose years of their lives, the freedom to move about in the world without debilitating fear, and any hope of returning to the pleasures of life as they once knew it.

People also fail to recognize that if a victim could not have anticipated an attack, she can have no assurance that she will be able to avoid one in the future. More to reassure themselves than to comfort the victim, some deny that such a thing could happen again. One friend, succumbing to the gambler's fallacy, pointed out that my having had such extraordinary bad luck meant that the odds of my being attacked again were now quite slim (as if fate, although not completely benign, would surely give me a break now, perhaps in the interest of fairness). Others thought it would be most comforting to act as if nothing had happened. The first card I received from my mother, while I was still in the hospital, made no mention of the attack or of my pain and featured the "bluebird of happiness," sent to keep me ever cheerful. The second had an illustration of a bright, summery scene with the greeting: "Isn't the sun nice? Isn't the wind nice? Isn't everything nice?" Weeks passed before I learned, what I should have been able to guess, that after she and my father received Tom's first call from the hospital they held each other and sobbed. They didn't want to burden me with their pain—a pain that I now realize must have been greater than my own.

Some devout relatives were quick to give God all the credit for my survival but none of the blame for what I had to endure. Others acknowledged the suffering that had been inflicted on me, but as no more than a blip on the graph of God's benevolence—necessary, fleeting, evil, there to make possible an even greater show of good. An aunt, with whom I had been close since childhood, did not write or call at all until three months after the attack, and then sent a belated birthday card with a note saying that she was sorry to hear about my "horrible experience" but pleased to think that as a result I "will become stronger and will be able to help so many people. A real blessing from above for sure." Such attempts at a theodicy discounted the horror I had to endure. But I learned that everyone needs to try and make sense, in however inadequate a way, of such senseless violence. I watched my own seesawing attempts to find something for which to be grateful, something to redeem the unmitigated awfulness: I was glad I didn't have to reproach myself (or endure others' reproaches) for having done something careless, but I wished I had done something I could consider reckless so that I could simply refrain from doing it in the future. For some time I was glad I did not yet have a child, who would have to grow up with the knowledge that even the protector could not be protected, but I felt an inexpressible loss when I recalled how much Tom and I had wanted a baby and how joyful were our attempts to conceive. It was difficult to imagine getting pregnant, because it was so hard to let even my husband near me, and because I felt it would be harder still to let a child leave my side.

It might be gathered, from this litany of complaints, that I was the recipient of constant, if misguided, attempts at consolation during the first few months of my recovery. This was not the case. It seemed to me that the half-life of most people's concern was less than that of the sleeping pills I took to ward off flashbacks and nightmares—just long enough to allow the construction of a comforting illusion that lulls the shock to sleep. During the first few months after my assault, my close friends, my sister, and my parents were supportive, but most of the aunts, uncles, cousins, and friends of the family notified by my parents almost immediately after the attack didn't phone, write, or even send a get well card, in spite of my extended hospital stay. These are all caring, decent people who would have sent wishes for a speedy recovery if I'd had, say, an appendectomy. Their early lack of response was so striking that I wondered whether it was the result of self-protective denial, a reluctance to mention something so unspeakable, or a symptom of our society's widespread emotional illiteracy that prevents most people from conveying any feeling that can't be expressed in a Hallmark card.

In the case of rape, the intersection of multiple taboos—against talking openly about trauma, about violence, about sex—causes conversational gridlock, paralyzing the would-be supporter. We lack the vocabulary for expressing appropriate concern, and we have no social conventions to ease the awkwardness. Ronald de Sousa (1987) has written persuasively about the importance of grasping paradigm scenarios in early childhood in order to learn appropriate emotional responses to situations. We do not learn—early or later in life—how to react to a rape. What typically results from this ignorance is bewilderment on the part of victims and silence on the part of others, often the result of misguided caution. When, on entering the angry phase of my recovery period, I railed at my parents: "Why haven't my relatives called or written? Why hasn't my own brother phoned?" They replied, "They all expressed their concern to us, but they didn't want to remind you of what happened."

Didn't they realize I thought about the attack every minute of every day and that their inability to respond made me feel as though I had, in fact, died and no one had bothered to come to the funeral?

For the next several months, I felt angry, scared, and helpless, and I wished I could blame myself for what had happened so that I would feel less vulnerable, more in control of my life. Those who haven't been sexually violated may have difficulty understanding why women who survive assault often blame themselves, and may wrongly attribute it to a sex-linked trait of masochism or lack of self-esteem. They don't know that it can be less painful to believe that you did something blameworthy than it is to think that you live in a world where you can be attacked at any time, in any place, simply because you are a woman. It is hard to go on after an attack that is both random—and thus completely unpredictable—and not random, that is, a crime of hatred toward the group to which you happen to belong. If I hadn't been the one who was attacked on that road in France, it would have been the next woman to come along. But had my husband walked down that road instead, he would have been safe.

Although I didn't blame myself for the attack, neither could I blame my attacker. Tom wanted to kill him, but I, like other rape victims I came to know, found it almost impossible to get angry with my assailant. I think the terror I still felt precluded the appropriate angry response. It may be that experiencing anger toward an attacker requires imagining oneself in proximity to him, a prospect too frightening for a victim in the early stages of recovery to conjure up. As Aristotle observed in the *Rhetoric*, Book I, "no one grows angry with a person on whom there is no prospect of taking vengeance, and we feel comparatively little anger, or none at all, with those who are much our superiors in power."[8] The anger was still there, but it got directed toward safer targets: my family and closest friends. My anger spread, giving me painful shooting signs that I was coming back to life. I could not accept what had happened to me. What was I supposed to do now? How could everyone else carry on with their lives when women were dying? How could Tom go on teaching his classes, seeing students, chatting with colleagues . . . and why should he be able to walk down the street when I couldn't?

The incompatibility of fear of my assailant and appropriate anger toward him became most apparent after I began taking a women's self-defense class. It became clear that the way to break out of the double bind of self-blame versus powerlessness was through empowerment—physical as well as political. Learning to fight back is a crucial part of this process, not only because it enables us to experience justified, healing rage, but also because, as Iris Young has observed in her essay "Throwing Like a Girl," "women in sexist society are physically handicapped," moving about hesitantly, fearfully, in a constricted lived space, routinely underestimating what strength we actually have (Young 1990, 153). We have to learn to feel entitled to occupy space, to defend ourselves. The hardest thing for most of the women in my self-defense class to do was simply to yell "No!" Women have been taught not to fight back when being attacked, to rely instead on placating or pleading with one's assailant—strategies that researchers have found to be least effective in resisting rape (Bart and O'Brien 1984).

The instructor of the class, Linda Ramzy Ranson, helped me through the difficult first sessions, through the flashbacks and the fear, and showed me I could be tougher than ever. As I was leaving after one session, I saw a student arrive for the next class—with a guide dog. I was furious that, in addition to everything else this woman had to struggle with, she had to worry about being raped. I thought I understood something of her fear since I felt, for the first time in my life, like I had a perceptual deficit—not the blurred vision from the detached vitreous, but, rather, the more hazardous lack of eyes in the back of my head. I tried to compensate for this on my walks by looking over my shoulder a lot and punctuating my purposeful, straight-ahead stride with an occasional pirouette, which must have made me look more whimsical than terrified.

The confidence I gained from learning how to fight back effectively not only enabled me to walk down the street again, it gave me back my life. But it was a changed life. A paradoxical life. I began to feel stronger than ever before, and more vulnerable, more determined to fight to change the world, but in need of several naps a day. News that friends found distressing in a less visceral way—the racism and sexism in the coverage of the trials of the defendants in the Central Park jogger case and in the trial of the St. John's gang-rape defendants, the rape and murder of Kimberly Rae Harbour in Boston in October 1990 (virtually ignored by the media since the victim was black), the controversy over *American Psycho*, the Gulf War, the Kennedy rape case, the Tyson trial, the fatal stabbing of law professor Mary Joe Frug near Harvard Square, the ax murders of two women graduate students at Dartmouth College (also neglected by all but the local press since the victims were black and from Ethiopia)—triggered debilitating flashbacks in me. Unlike survivors of wars or earthquakes, who inhabit a common shattered world, rape victims face the cataclysmic destruction of their world alone, surrounded by people who find it hard to understand what's so distressing. I realized that I exhibited every symptom of post-traumatic stress disorder—dissociation, flashbacks, hypervigilance, exaggerated startle response, sleep disorders, inability to concentrate, diminished interest in significant activities, and a sense of a foreshortened future.[10] I could understand why children exposed to urban violence have such trouble envisioning their futures. Although I had always been career-oriented, always planning for my future, I could no longer imagine how I would get through each day, let alone what I might be doing in a year's time. I didn't think I would ever write or teach philosophy again.

The American Psychiatric Association's *Diagnostic and Statistical Manual* defines post-traumatic stress disorder, in part, as the result of "an event that is outside the range of usual human experience."[11] Because the trauma is, to most people, inconceivable, it's also unspeakable. Even when I managed to find the words and the strength to describe my ordeal, it was hard for others to hear about it. They would have preferred me to just "buck up," as one friend urged me to do. But it's essential to talk about it, again and again. It's a way of remastering the trauma, although it can be retraumatizing when people refuse to listen. In my case, each time someone failed to respond I felt as though I were alone again in the ravine, dying, screaming. And still no one could hear me. Or, worse, they heard me, but refused to help.

I now know they were trying to help, but that recovering from trauma takes time, patience, and, most of all, determination on the part of the survivor. After about six months, I began to be able to take more responsibility for my own recovery, and stopped expecting others to pull me through. I entered the final stage of my recovery, a period of gradual acknowledgment and integration of what had happened. I joined a rape survivors' support group, I got a great deal of therapy, and I became involved in political activities, such as promoting the Violence against Women Act (which was eventually passed by Congress in 1994).[12] Gradually, I was able to get back to work.

When I resumed teaching at Dartmouth in the fall of 1991, the first student who came to see me in my office during freshman orientation week told me that she had been raped. The following spring, four Dartmouth students reported sexual assaults to the local police. In the aftermath of these recent reports, the women students on my campus were told to use their heads, lock their doors, not go out after dark without a male escort. They were advised: just don't do anything stupid.

Although colleges are eager to "protect" women by hindering their freedom of movement or providing them with male escorts, they continue to be reluctant to teach women how to protect themselves. After months of lobbying the administration at my college, we were able to convince them to offer a women's self-defense and rape prevention course. It was offered in the winter of 1992 as a physical education course, and nearly a hundred students and employees signed up for it. Shortly after the course began, I was informed that the women students were not going to be allowed to get P.E.

credit for it, since the administration had determined that it discriminated against men. I was told that granting credit for the course was in violation of Title IX, which prohibits sex discrimination in education programs receiving federal funding—even though granting credit to men for being on the football team was not, even though Title IX law makes an explicit exception for P.E. classes involving substantial bodily contact, and even though every term the college offers several martial arts courses, for credit, that are open to men, geared to men's physiques and needs, and taken predominantly by men. I was told by an administrator that, even if Title IX permitted it, offering a women's self-defense course for credit violated "the College's non-discrimination clause—a clause which, I hope, all reasonable men and women support as good policy."

The implication that I was not a "reasonable woman" didn't sit well with me as a philosopher, so I wrote a letter to the appropriate administrative committee criticizing my college's position that single-sex sports, male-only fraternities, female-only sororities, and pregnancy leave policies are not discriminatory, in any invidious sense, while a women's self-defense class is. The administration finally agreed to grant P.E. credit for the course, but shortly after that battle was over, I read in the New York Times that "a rape prevention ride service offered to women in the city of Madison and on the University of Wisconsin campus may lose its university financing because it discriminates against men."[13] The dean of students at Wisconsin said that this group—the Women's Transit Authority—which has been providing free nighttime rides to women students for nineteen years, must change its policy to allow male drivers and passengers. These are, in my view, examples of the application of what Catharine MacKinnon refers to as "the stupid theory of equality."[14] To argue that rape prevention policies for women discriminate against men is like arguing that money spent making university buildings more accessible to disabled persons discriminates against those able-bodied persons who do not benefit from these improvements.[15]

Sexual violence victimizes not only those women who

are directly attacked, but *all* women. The fear of rape has long functioned to keep women in their place. Whether or not one agrees with the claims of those, such as Susan Brownmiller (1995), who argue that rape is a means by which *all* men keep *all* women subordinate, the fact that all women's lives are restricted by sexual violence is indisputable. The authors of *The Female Fear*, Margaret Gordon and Stephanie Riger, cite studies substantiating what every woman already knows—that the fear of rape prevents women from enjoying what men consider to be their birthright. Fifty percent of women never use public transportation after dark because of fear of rape. Women are eight times more likely than men to avoid walking in their own neighborhoods after dark, for the same reason (Gordon and Riger 1991). In the seminar on Violence against Women that I taught for the first time in the spring of 1992, the men in the class were stunned by the extent to which the women in the class took precautions against assault every day—locking doors and windows, checking the back seat of the car, not walking alone at night, looking in closets on returning home. And this is at a "safe," rural New England campus.

Although women still have their work and leisure opportunities unfairly restricted by their relative lack of safety, paternalistic legislation excluding women from some of the "riskier" forms of employment (e.g., bartending)[16] has, thankfully, disappeared, except, that is, in the military. We are still debating whether women should be permitted to engage in combat, and the latest rationale for keeping women out of battle is that they are more vulnerable than men to sexual violence. Those wanting to limit women's role in the military have used the reported indecent assaults on two female American prisoners of war in Iraq as evidence for women's unsuitability for combat.[17] One might as well argue that the fact that women are much more likely than men to be sexually assaulted on college campuses is evidence that women are not suited to post-secondary education. No one, to my knowledge, has proposed returning Ivy League colleges to their former all-male status as a solution to the problem of campus rape. Some have, however, seriously proposed enacting after-dark curfews for women, in spite of the fact that men are the perpetrators of the assaults. This is yet another indication of how natural it still seems to many people to address the problem of sexual violence by curtailing women's lives. The absurdity of this approach becomes apparent once one realizes that a woman can be sexually assaulted anywhere, at any time—in "safe" places, in broad daylight, even in her own home.

For months after my assault, I was afraid of people finding out about it—afraid of their reactions and of their inability to respond. I was afraid that my professional work would be discredited, that I would be viewed as biased, or, even worse, not properly philosophical. Now I am no longer afraid of what might happen if I speak out about sexual violence. I'm much more afraid of what will continue to happen if I don't. Sexual violence is a problem of catastrophic proportions—a fact obscured by its mundanity, by its relentless occurrence, by the fact that so many of us have been victims of it. Imagine the moral outrage, the emergency response we would surely mobilize, if all of these everyday assaults occurred at the same time or were restricted to one geographical region. But why should the spatiotemporal coordinates of the vast numbers of sexual assaults be considered to be morally relevant? From the victim's point of view, the fact that she is isolated in her rape and her recovery, combined with the ordinariness of the crime that leads to its trivialization, makes the assault and its aftermath even more traumatic.

As devastating as sexual violence is, however, I want to stress that it is possible to survive it, and even to flourish after it, although it doesn't seem that way at the time. Whenever I see a survivor struggling with the overwhelming anger and sadness, I'm reminded of a sweet, motherly, woman in my rape survivors' support group who sat silently throughout the group's first meeting. At the end of the hour she finally asked, softly, through tears: "Can anyone tell me if it ever stops hurting?" At the time I had the same question, and wasn't satisfied with any answer. Now I can say, yes, it does stop hurting, at least for longer periods of time. A year after my assault, I was pleased to discover that I could go for fifteen minutes without thinking about it. Now I can go for hours at a stretch without a flashback. That's on a good day. On a bad day, I may still take to my bed with lead in my veins, unable to find one good reason to go on.

Our group facilitator, Ann Gaulin, told us that first meeting: "You will never be the same. But you can be better." I protested that I had lost so much: my security, my self-esteem, my love, and my work. I had been happy with the way things were. How could they ever be better now? As a survivor, she knew how I felt, but she also knew that, as she put it, "When your life is shattered, you're forced to pick up the pieces, and you have a chance to stop and examine them. You can say 'I don't want this one anymore' or 'I think I'll work on that one.'" I have had to give up more than I would ever have chosen to. But I have gained important skills and insights, and I no longer feel tainted by my victimization. Granted, those of us who live through sexual assault aren't given ticker-tape parades or the keys to our cities, but it's an honor to be a survivor. Although it's not exactly the sort of thing I can put on my résumé, it's the accomplishment of which I'm most proud.

Two years after the assault, I could speak about it in a philosophical forum. There I could acknowledge the good things that came from the recovery process—the clarity, the confidence, the determination, the many supporters and survivors who had brought meaning back into my world. This was not to say that the attack and its aftermath were, on balance, a good thing or, as my aunt put it, "a real blessing from above." I would rather not have gone down that road. It has been hard for me, as a philosopher, to learn the lesson that knowledge isn't always desirable, that the truth doesn't always set you free. Sometimes, it fills you with incapacitating terror and, then, uncontrollable rage. But I suppose you should embrace it anyway, for the reason Nietzsche exhorts you to love your enemies: if it doesn't kill you, it makes you stronger.

People ask me if I'm recovered now, and I reply that it depends on what that means. If they mean "am I back to where I was before the attack?" I have to say, no, and I never will be. I am not the same person who set off, singing, on that sunny Fourth of July in the French countryside. I left her in a rocky creek bed at the bottom of a ravine. I had to in order to survive. I understand the appropriateness of what a friend described to me as a Jewish custom of giving those who have outlived a brush with death new names. The trauma has changed me forever, and if I insist too often that my friends and family acknowledge it, that's because I'm afraid they don't know who I am.

But if recovery means being able to incorporate this awful knowledge into my life and carry on, then, yes, I'm recovered. I don't wake up each day with a start, thinking, "This can't have happened to me!" It happened. I have no guarantee that it won't happen again, although my self-defense classes have given me the confidence to move about in the world and to go for longer and longer walks—with my two big dogs. Sometimes I even manage to enjoy myself. And I no longer cringe when I see a woman jogging alone on the country road where I live, although I may still have a slight urge to rush out and protect her, to tell her to come inside where she'll be safe. But I catch myself, like a mother learning to let go, and cheer her on, thinking, may she always be so carefree, so at home in her world. She has every right to be.

The free intellect will see as God might see, without a
here and *now*, without hopes and fears, without the
trammels of customary beliefs and traditional prejudices,
calmly, dispassionately, in the sole and exclusive desire
of knowledge—knowledge as impersonal, as purely
contemplative, as it is possible for man to attain. Hence
also the free intellect will value more the abstract and
universal knowledge into which the accidents of private
history do not enter, than the knowledge brought by the
senses, and dependent, as such knowledge must be,
upon an exclusive and personal point of view and a body
whose sense-organs distort as much as they reveal.
—Bertrand Russell, *The Problems of Philosophy*[1]

Gradually it has become clear to me what every great
philosophy so far has been: namely the personal
confession of its author and a kind of involuntary and
unconscious memoir.
—Friedrich Nietzsche, *Beyond Good and Evil*[2]

On the Personal as Philosophical

CHAPTER   TWO

Russell's *Problems of Philosophy* was one of the first philosophy texts I read, and I was so drawn to the idea of knowledge as "impersonal, . . . abstract and universal" that it has taken me nearly twenty years to come to see, gradually, the appeal of Nietzsche's view of philosophy as a kind of disguised autobiographical narrative. I was aware that, for centuries, philosophers had written in the first-person singular, but the "serious" ones, such as Descartes, did so as part of an argumentative strategy to be employed by any reader to establish, ultimately, the same universal truths. They weren't *really* talking about themselves. As we so often tell beginning students of philosophy who attempt to defend positions by writing "I feel that . . . " or "I think that . . . ," such self-descriptions have no place in philosophical argumentation. What the reader, that is, the professor, wants to know is not what this particular author happens to feel or think—and why—but, rather, what reasons *any* rational person has to accept the position in question. Those "accidents of private history," disparaged by Russell, must be put out of one's mind if one is to "see as God might see, without a *here* and *now.*"

Now of course Russell, like Nietzsche, was an atheist, so it is a bit of a mystery why he thought human beings could accomplish feats of this sort which, when attributed to God, made the idea of such a Being incredible. But many, perhaps most, mainstream analytic philosophers writing today share Russell's view and consider the search for timeless, acontextual truths to be the sine qua non of the philosophical enterprise.

However, some philosophers—even some trained in the analytic tradition as I was (and by this I mean Anglo-American, not psychoanalytic!)—have come to reject this view. Many feminist philosophers agree with Virginia Held that "[t]he philosophical tradition that has purported to present the view of the essentially and universally human has, masked by this claim, presented instead a view that is masculine, white, and Western" (1993, 19). Having acquainted ourselves with feminist theorizing as it is carried out in other disciplines, we are finding the traditional philosophical obsession with the impersonal and acontextual increasingly indefensible. As we find that the "accidents of private history," especially those connected with gender, race, ethnicity, religion, sexuality, and class, are not only worth thinking about, but are also inevitably, even if invisibly, present in much of philosophy, we are beginning to write in the first person, not out of sloppy self-indulgence, but out of intellectual necessity.

Feminist ethics, in particular, in accepting subjective accounts as legitimate means of advancing knowledge, has made it *somewhat* more academically acceptable to write in the personal voice. In questioning the dichotomy between the personal and the political, and in insisting on the relevance of particular women's actual experiences, feminist methodology can reveal the bias in the exclusion of rape and other forms of sexual violence from the traditional concerns of ethics. As Held observes, whereas "[t]raditional moral theory is frequently built on what a person might be thought to hold from the point of view of a hypothetical ideal observer, or a hypothetical purely rational being," feminist ethics relies on the actual experiences of concrete individuals, paying special attention to the formerly neglected experiences of women and other marginalized groups. (1993, 34) Feminist theorists are increasingly looking to first-person accounts to gain imaginative access to others' experiences. Such access can facilitate empathy with others, which is valued by many feminist theorists as a method of moral understanding needed to complement more detached analytical reasoning.

The "accident of private history" that forced me to think about the "personal" as philosophical was a near-fatal sexual assault and attempted murder. Unlike Descartes, who had "to demolish everything completely and start again right from the foundations" in order to find any knowledge "that was stable and likely to last," I had my world demolished for me.[3] The fact that I could be walking down a quiet, sunlit country road at one moment and be battling a murderous

attacker the next undermined my most fundamental assumptions about the world. After my hospitalization, I took
a year-long disability leave from teaching and found myself,
like Descartes, "quite alone," with "a clear stretch of free
time" in which to rebuild my shattered system of beliefs.[4]

As I carried out this process of cognitive, as well as
physical and emotional, recovery, I was dismayed to find
very little of use to me that was written by philosophers. It
occurred to me that the fact that rape was not considered a
properly philosophical subject, while war, for example, was,
resulted not only from the paucity of women in the profession but also from the disciplinary bias against thinking
about the 'personal,' against writing in the form of narrative.
(Of course, the avowedly personal experiences of *men* have
been neglected in philosophical analysis as well. The study of
the ethics of war, for example, has dealt with questions of
strategy and justice, as viewed from the outside, and not
with the wartime *experiences* of soldiers or with the aftermath of their trauma.)[5]

In philosophy, first-person narratives, especially ones
written by those with perspectives previously excluded from
the discipline, are necessary for several reasons. I'll discuss
just three. Such narratives are necessary: (1) to expose previously hidden biases in the discipline's subject matter and
methodology; (2) to facilitate understanding of (or empathy
with) those different from ourselves; and (3) to lay on the
table our own biases as scholars.

First-person narratives can expose the gender and other
biases inherent in, among other things, much traditional
moral, legal, and political philosophy. They can serve to bear
witness, bringing professional attention to the injustices suffered by previously neglected or discounted groups. Such
narratives can also provide the basis for empathy with those
who are different from ourselves, which, as recently argued
by feminist moral theorists such as Diana Meyers, is crucial
for an adequately inclusive understanding of certain moral,
legal, and political issues.[6]

In other fields, as well, first-person accounts can facilitate the understanding of cultural attitudes and practices different from our own, as Renato Rosaldo has argued (and shown) in "Grief and a Headhunter's Rage."[7] In this chapter, Rosaldo, an anthropologist who had previously published a book on headhunting among the Ilongot (in the Philippines), describes how the experience of rage after the death of his wife, Michelle Rosaldo, gave him new insight into the rage Ilongot older men felt in bereavement. Before his own encounter with grief, Rosaldo writes, he "brushed aside" Ilongot accounts of "the rage in bereavement that could impel men to headhunt." He says he probably "naively equated grief with sadness." Only after "being repositioned" by his own "devastating loss" could he begin to grasp that "Ilongot older men mean precisely what they say when they describe the anger in bereavement as the source of their desire to cut off human heads."[8] This is not to say that he fully comprehended (or condoned) the past headhunting behavior of the Ilongots, but it became less foreign to him. His first-person narrative, likewise, makes the practice less foreign to us, his readers. As he explains, his "use of personal experience serves as a vehicle for making the quality and intensity of the rage in Ilongot grief more readily accessible to readers than certain more detached modes of composition."[9]

At other times, first-person narratives are used simply to put on the table one's perspectives and possible biases, which of course implies the acknowledgment that such things inevitably work their way into our research, no matter how scrupulously "objective" we try to be. Susan Estrich begins her book, *Real Rape*, with an account of the rape she survived in 1974. To justify this radical and courageous introduction to a long-neglected legal subject, Estrich argues that if the rape wasn't her fault, if she's not ashamed, why shouldn't she mention it? "And so I mention it. I mention it in my classes. I describe it here. I do so in the interest of full disclosure. I like to think that I am an informed and intelligent student of rape. But I am not unbiased. I am no objective observer, if such a thing exists (which I doubt; I think the major difference between me and those who have written 'objectively' about the law of rape is that I admit my involvement and bias). In writing about rape, I am writing about my own life" (pp. 1–3).

As Held observes, feminists who doubt "that anyone can truly reflect the essentially and universally human, and [are] suspicious of those who presume to do so, . . . often ask that speakers openly acknowledge the backgrounds from which they speak so that their hearers can better understand the contexts of the experiences" (p. 19). In her recent book, *Feminist Morality,* Held overcomes her own "pyschological inclination" and philosophical training and describes her personal and intellectual background, acknowledging explicitly that the feminist views presented in her book are not reflective of a wider range of feminist thinking, but rather emerge from her own "philosophical background and experience" (pp. 19–21). Likewise, in her book, *Moral Prejudices,* Annette Baier includes a discussion of her development in the profession as a feminist philosopher as well as a series of anecdotes about her experiences as a woman in a world in which trusting certain men can be dangerous. In her defense of these unusual philosophical moves, she acknowledges, "I know, however, that I will not convince many of my fellow moral philosophers" of their appropriateness, given that "[t]he impersonal style has become nearly a sacred tradition in moral philosophy" (p. 194). But to her credit she is not dissuaded by comments such as the one proffered by a "respected older mentor" after she gave a talk employing such anecdotes about trust: "This may all be great fun, but is it real professional work?" (p. 328, n.20).

The above theorists who employ the personal voice all recognize a fundamental characteristic of feminist theory, which is that it takes women's experiences seriously. Likewise, trauma theory takes survivors' experiences seriously. And we cannot know what these are a priori. We need to tell our stories, making sure to listen to those of others, especially when they're at odds with ours.

First-person narratives in feminist philosophy and in

trauma theory may seem to be of the same genre as Descartes' *Meditations*, but, in spite of having superficially similar narrative structures, they differ radically in their intellectual aims. Feminists and trauma theorists writing of their own experiences do not claim, as did Descartes, that any rational person carrying out the same line of abstract reasoning will reach the same impersonal conclusions. Rather, we are suggesting that anyone in these particular circumstances, with this kind of socialization, with these options and limitations may (*may*, not must) view the world in this way. If first-person narratives are to help serve as an antidote to the obliteration of difference in theory, they must avoid the risk of overgeneralization.

Theorizing in the personal voice is not without its hazards, as the above discussion of the importance of acknowledging one's biases points out, but I think that with care they can be largely avoided by those writing and reading such narratives. At the very least, they can be noted. They include: (1) the dilemma of speaking only for oneself versus speaking, without warrant, on behalf of a larger group; (2) taking statements of experience or remembered experiences at face value, as foundational; (3) generating (unjustified) counter-narratives of victimization; and (4) perpetuating negative stereotypes about one's group and contributing to the sensationalizing or the trivializing of the group's experience of victimization.

The theorist who uses her own narrative of trauma or of victimization in her scholarship faces the dilemma, on the one hand, of speaking only for herself, giving in to self-indulgence or speaking about experiences so idiosyncratic that her narrative is of no use to others or, on the other hand, of presuming to speak for all members of a group to which she belongs (e.g., all trauma survivors, all rape survivors, all white female American middle-class heterosexual rape survivors). No matter how carefully the group is delineated, she runs the risk of overgeneralizing (as well as undergeneralizing). Although a survivor experiences, remembers, and narrates trauma *as* a member of *at least one* group, such a narrative should not be taken, in isolation, as standard for victimized members of that group. Furthermore, we need to rethink our (all or nothing) assumptions about identity, acknowledging the complexities of our multiple identities.[10]

The hazard of presuming to speak for all members of a group, for example, for all women (something white, middle-class academic feminists have been all too prone to do), can be avoided, at least to some extent, by making clear the background from which one writes and refraining from overgeneralizing in one's conclusions. Through my participation in a survivors' support group as well as in the anti-rape movement I discovered the many ways in which my race (white) and class (middle), in addition to my academic preoccupations, had distanced me from the concerns of many other victims of sexual violence. Although all of us in the support group (in center-city Philadelphia) had been raped, and we shared the symptoms of post-traumatic stress disorder, these symptoms had a more devastating effect on some of us than on others, because of our different backgrounds and present circumstances. I wondered about whether I would ever be able to function well enough to resume my teaching and research, while others worried about finding housing for themselves and their children, or about getting off drugs, or about dealing with our racist legal system that does not take black rape victims as seriously as white ones, or about supporting themselves (since they'd worked the night shift and were now too afraid to take public transportation to work after dark). We all struggled to get from one day to the next, but our struggles were not the same.

But we need not speak *for* other survivors of trauma in order to speak *with* them.

A second pitfall is that of taking experiences and narrated memories of subjective experiences at face value, as given or foundational. As Andreas Huyssen notes, "The past is not simply there in memory, but it must be articulated to become memory. The fissure that opens up between experiencing an event and remembering it in representation is unavoidable."[11] The tendency to take certain memories—traumatic memories—as simply given, and retained as snapshots, exists in trauma theory, when a distinction is made between traumatic memories (viewed as bodily, fragmented, sensory, intrusive, recurrent, uncontrollable) and narrative memories (viewed as linguistic, more coherent, more under control). Traumatic memory, like narrative memory, is articulated, selective, even malleable, in spite of the fact that the framing of such memory may not be under the survivor's conscious control.

Furthermore, I would add to Huyssens' observation of the gap between experience and memory that there is, in addition, a gap between the event (which may be described in countless ways) and the experience of it. I am here simply rejecting a naive realist view of perception and of experience generally, a view that may be unwittingly evoked by those trauma theorists who emphasize the "snapshot" character of traumatic memory. (Not even *snapshots* capture "the given" as it is, without distortion and selection.)[12] Events are experienced by means of representations—sensory perceptions, bodily sensations, and linguistic classification (even if only as "something terrifying"), and these are all influenced by the perceived cultural meanings of the events. As Maurice Halbwachs observes, "it is in society that people acquire their memories" (1992, 38). I would add that this is so even when people are alone at the time the memories are acquired. "It is also in society that they recall, recognize, and localize their memories" (1992, 38), Halbwachs continues, and, again, I would add, even when they are alone during the process.

How one experiences a trauma, for example, depends on how one (often unconsciously) categorizes the event: is it life-threatening, is it human-inflicted, is it inescapable? These categorizations (which depend on the culturally available models and metaphors) determine whether one feels fear, anger, hopelessness, or other seemingly unmediated emotions.

I recall first experiencing my assault as an incomprehensible random event, surely a nightmare (a reversal of the epistemological crisis provoked by Descartes' question, "What if I'm dreaming?" Instead, I asked myself in desperation, "What if I'm awake?"). When the sexual nature of the assault became apparent, I experienced it as a rape ("Oh, so *that's* what this is") and tried to recall all I'd heard about what one is supposed to do in such a situation. When, after I "woke up," subsequent to being strangled into unconsciousness, and I realized that I was being treated as a corpse (my assailant was dragging me by my feet to a creek bed at the bottom of a steep ravine), I redescribed the event as "a murder-in-progress." Each new categorization of the assault affected my perception of my assailant and my strategies of defense. And each one inflects how I remember and would now describe the event: "I felt a sudden blow from behind, like being hit by a car." "I was a victim of gender-motivated sexual violence." "I survived a near-fatal murder attempt."

In light of these ways in which I experienced the traumatic event, I am puzzled by Cathy Caruth's (1996) discussion of trauma as an "unclaimed" or "missed experience." She writes that trauma is the result of "the lack of preparedness to take in a stimulus that comes too quickly. It is not simply, that is, the literal threatening of bodily life, but the fact that the threat is recognized as such by the mind *one moment too late*. The shock of the mind's relation to the threat of death is thus not the direct experience of the threat, but precisely the *missing* of this experience, the fact that, not being experienced *in time*, it has not yet been fully known" (1996, 62). There is a slippage, in Caruth's discussion, from a noting of the *lack of preparedness* for the threat of death to a claim that the experience of the threat of death is *missing*. This may be true in the case of some survivors, but research on trauma indicates that, at least in the case of a single traumatic event, the event is typically experienced at the time and remembered from that time, although the full emotional impact of the trauma takes time to absorb and work through.

Elizabeth Tonkin observes that "[t]he contents or evoked messages of memory are . . . ineluctably social insofar as they are acquired in the social world and can be coded in symbol systems which are culturally familiar" (1992, 112). The same can be said of experiences themselves. Joan Scott rightly rejects the "appeal to experience as uncontestable evidence and as an originary point of explanation—as a foundation upon which analysis is based" (1992, 24). Such an appeal to experience not only weakens "the critical thrust of histories of difference," as Scott notes, it also fails to capture the experience of experience.

Naomi Scheman (1983) has argued that even psychological states such as emotions are social constructs, which is not to say that anyone consciously constructs them nor that one can choose *not* to have them. As Scott puts it, "[s]ubjects are constituted discursively, experience is a linguistic event (it doesn't happen outside established meanings), but neither is it confined to a fixed order of meaning. Since discourse is by definition shared, experience is collective as well as individual" (1992, 34). It is important to note the parenthetical comment she makes after stating that "experience is a linguistic event." She writes, "(it doesn't happen outside established meanings)." She is not implying, as some postmodernist theorists are uncharitably accused of thinking, that experiences such as rape or torture don't really happen, or are all in the head, or all in the culture, or all in the terms used to describe them. Events happen. But they can be described in countless ways and they are experienced under some descriptions and not others.

This is to say more than simply that the experience must be viewed in context. Just as the experience is not simply given, neither is the context. Jonathan Culler's critique of the concept of context is useful here: "[T]he notion of context frequently oversimplifies rather than enriches discussion, since the opposition between an act [or experience, I would add] and its context seems to presume that the context is given and determines the meaning of the act. We know, of course, that things are not so simple: context is not fundamentally different from what it contextualizes; context is not given but produced; what belongs to a context is determined by interpretive strategies; contexts are just as much in need of elucidation as events; and the meaning of a context is determined by events."[13]

Keeping in mind these caveats against taking the experience, its context, or its memory as given, we can avoid a third hazard of first-person narratives of trauma and victimization, which is that they tend to generate competing narratives of victimization, not all of which are justified. Martha Minow points out that "victim talk" tends to provoke counter-"victim talk" (note the recent rhetoric of the "angry white male victim" of affirmative action) and not all these narratives can be taken at face value, since they are often at odds with one another.[14] Minow (1993, 1435) acknowledges that "[i]ndividualized stories are essential to avoid the dehumanizing abstractions that allow people to forget or trivialize the suffering of others." But she warns that "there is a risk that emphasizing individual stories and stressing feelings can undermine critical evaluation and analysis of contradictory claims." First-person narratives—of trauma or of other experiences of victimization—cannot be taken simply at face value. No testimony is incorrigible. If a claim of victimization is made on behalf of a group, for example, or because of one's membership in a group, the past and present victimization of the group in question needs to be critically examined.

If victims' stories are accepted as unassailable, unjustified reverse-victimization claims can be harder to contradict, with the ultimate effect that no victimization claim can be taken seriously. The solution to this problem is not to silence (or stop listening to) all those claiming to be victimized, but to allow ourselves to evaluate their claims, while bearing in mind and attempting to overcome the difficulties in understanding the experiences of those who are different from ourselves. In addition, since the perceptions of non-dominant groups have traditionally been considered "biased" to the extent that they depart from what is considered the norm, special efforts are required to evaluate them fairly. "Personal" stories must be framed by longer historical accounts and by broader social and political ones.

A fourth hazard of narrating group-based trauma is that, in doing so, one may inadvertently perpetuate stereotypes of one's group as weak and helpless. This can be the result of others' co-opting or trivializing the trauma. Although there is a risk, especially for victims of sexual violence, of having one's testimony distorted or neutralized, especially by the media (Alcoff and Gray 1993), it can be countered by rejecting the dichotomy between victimization and agency, avoiding sensationalistic accounts, and refraining from appearing on talk shows in which sleaze is valued over truth.

In addition to the above hazards, there is the professional risk, for those doing philosophy in the personal voice, of not being taken seriously (as in the comment by Baier's respected mentor) or (what probably amounts to the same thing in our discipline) not being taken philosophically. Although first-person narratives have for some time been considered academically respectable in literary and legal theory, in philosophy they are still usually dismissed as "just autobiography." This is a mistake. For the reasons discussed above, more first-person narratives are needed to help illuminate a variety of philosophical issues, including not only sexual violence, but also pornography, sexual harassment, pregnancy, abortion, new reproductive technologies, child care, welfare, war, and many other issues at the fraught intersections of gender, race, class, and sexual orientation.[15]

Shortly after my first article on sexual violence was published in 1993, I was told by a colleague: "Now you can put this behind you." But I know that I will never forget the assault and that it is a sign of recovered strength, not moral frailty or intellectual feebleness, that I am able to incorporate this awful knowledge into my work. It is no longer an option for me to follow Russell's advice and attempt to think "without a *here* and *now*, without hopes and fears." Instead, when I philosophize, I try to follow the example of Audre Lorde who, as Barbara Christian recalled, wrote with an "insistence on speaking as her entire self, whatever the consequences."[16]

I died in Auschwitz, but no one knows it.

—Charlotte Delbo[1]

Outliving Oneself

CHAPTER   THREE

Survivors of trauma frequently remark that they are not the same people they were before they were traumatized. As a survivor of the Nazi death camps observes, "One can be alive after Sobibor without having survived Sobibor."[2] Jonathan Shay, a therapist who works with Vietnam veterans, has often heard his patients say, "I died in Vietnam."[3] Migael Scherer expresses a loss commonly experienced by rape survivors when she writes, "I will always miss myself as I was."[4] What are we to make of these cryptic comments?[5] How can one miss oneself? How can one die in Vietnam or fail to survive a death camp and still live to tell one's story? How does a life-threatening event come to be experienced as self-annihilating? And what self is it who remembers having had this experience?

How one answers these questions depends on, among other things, how one defines "trauma" and "the self." In this chapter, I discuss the nature of trauma, show how it affects the self, construed in several ultimately interconnected ways, and then use this analysis to elaborate and support a feminist account of the relational self.[6] On this view the self is both autonomous and socially dependent, vulnerable enough to be undone by violence and yet resilient enough to be reconstructed with the help of empathic others.

My methodology differs from that used in traditional philosophizing about the self, and yields distinctly different results. Philosophers writing about the self have, at least since Locke, puzzled over such questions as whether persons can survive the loss or exchange of their minds, brains, consciousness, memories, characters, and/or bodies.[7] In recent years, increasingly gruesome and high-tech thought experiments involving fusion, fission, freezing, dissolution, reconstitution, and/or teletransportation of an individual have been devised to test our intuitions about who, if anyone, survives which permutations.[8] Given philosophers' preoccupation with personal identity in extreme, life-threatening, and possibly self-annihilating situations, it is odd that they have neglected to consider the accounts of actual trauma victims who report that they are not the same people they were prior to their traumatic transformations.[9] This oversight may result from the fact that imaginary scenarios, however far-fetched, are at least *conceivable*, whereas the experiences of rape victims, Holocaust survivors, and war veterans are, for most of us, unthinkable. In addition, philosophers are trained to divert their gaze from the messy real world to the neater, more controllable, and more comprehensible realm of pure thought.

As I discussed in the previous chapter, however, feminist theorists writing in the areas of ethics and social, political, and legal philosophy have recently argued for the necessity of focusing on the actual experiences of real people and have made use of first- and third-person narratives in their attempts to do this.[10] Feminist theorists have also stressed the importance of taking context into account, recognizing that we all reason from a "positioned perspective" and that some of us, with "multiple consciousness," reason from a variety of sometimes incompatible perspectives.[11] In addition, feminist theorists have adopted interdisciplinary approaches to subjects, such as personal identity, previously thought to be the exclusive domain of one discipline. I use these feminist methodologies here, incorporating survivor testimonies, situating philosophical questions of the self in the context of actual individuals' lives, acknowledging my own perspective as a survivor, and drawing on the clinical literature on trauma.

Trauma and the Undoing of the Self

There is a much clearer professional consensus among psychologists about what counts as a traumatic event than there is among philosophers concerning the nature of the self.[12] A traumatic event is one in which a person feels utterly helpless in the face of a force that is perceived to be life-threatening.[13] The immediate psychological responses to such trauma include terror, loss of control, and intense fear of annihilation. Long-term effects include the physiological responses of hypervigilance, heightened startle response, sleep disorders, and the more psychological, yet still involuntary, responses of depression, inability to concentrate, lack of interest in activities that used to give life meaning, and a sense of a foreshortened future. A commonly accepted explanation of these symptoms of post-traumatic stress disorder (PTSD) is that, in trauma, the ordinarily adaptive human responses to danger that prepare the body to fight or flee are of no avail. "When neither resistance nor escape is possible," Judith Herman explains, "the human system of self-defense becomes overwhelmed and disorganized. Each component of the ordinary response to danger, having lost its utility, tends to persist in an altered and exaggerated state long after the actual danger is over" (Herman 1992, 34). When the trauma is of human origin and is intentionally inflicted, the kind I discuss in this book, it not only shatters one's fundamental assumptions about the world and one's safety in it, but it also severs the sustaining connection between the self and the rest of humanity. Victims of human-inflicted trauma are reduced to mere objects by their tormenters: their subjectivity is rendered useless and viewed as worthless. As Herman observes, "The traumatic event thus destroys the belief that one can *be oneself* in relation to others" (Herman 1992, 53). Without this belief, I argue, one can no longer *be oneself* even to oneself, since the self exists fundamentally in relation to others.

How one defines "self" depends in part on what explanatory work one wants the concept of a self to do. Philosophers have invoked this concept in various areas of the discipline in order to account for a wide range of phenomena. The self is, in metaphysics, whatever it is whose persistence accounts for personal identity over time. One metaphysical view of the self holds that it is bodily continuity that accounts for personal identity and the other, that it is continuity of memory, character traits, or other psychological characteristics that makes someone the same person over time. There is also the view, held by poststructuralists, that the self is a narrative, which, properly construed, is a version of the view that psychological continuity constitutes personal identity.[14] In ethics the self is viewed as the locus of autonomous agency and responsibility and, hence, is the subject of praise or blame. Most traditional accounts of the self, from Descartes' to contemporary theorists', have been individualistic, based on the assumption that one can individuate selves and determine the criteria for their identity over time independent of the social context in which they are situated. In contrast, feminist accounts of the self have focused on the ways in which the self is formed in relation to others and sustained in a social context. On these accounts, persons are, in Annette Baier's words, "second persons," that is, "essentially successors, heirs to other persons who formed and cared for them."[15] In addition, the self is viewed as related to and constructed by others in an ongoing way, not only bcause others continue to shape and define us throughout our lifetimes, but also because our own sense of self is couched in descriptions whose meanings are social phenomena (Scheman 1983).

In what follows, I argue that the study of trauma reveals that the accounts of the embodied self, the self as narrative, and the autonomous self are compatible and complementary, focusing on different aspects of the self. I also argue that the study of trauma provides additional support for the view that each of these aspects of the self is fundamentally relational.

The Embodied Self

Although we recognize other persons most readily by their perceptible, that is, bodily, attributes, philosophers have been loath to identify the self with a body for a host of reasons.[16] A dead body cannot be said to be anyone's self, nor can a living, but permanently comatose, one. We do not typically use a bodily criterion of identity to determine who we ourselves are, and most of us, when imagining Locke's prince, whose soul "enters and informs" the body of a cobbler, would suppose the resulting person to be the prince

—

Outliving
Oneself

(Locke 1974, 216). Some philosophers[17] have been concerned to show that the self can survive the death of the body, but perhaps the primary reason philosophers have not identified the self with the body is an ancient bias against our physical nature.[18] Plato praised philosophers for "despising the body and avoiding it," and urged that "[i]f we are ever to have pure knowledge of anything, we must get rid of the body and contemplate things by themselves with the soul by itself."[19] This rejection of the body has been most apparent in the disparaging of the female body, which has been presented as the antithesis to reason. Although, as Sara Ruddick notes, "[t]here is nothing intrinsically masculine about mind and objectivity or anything feminine about passion and physicality, . . . philosophers have tended to associate, explicitly or metaphorically, passion, affection, and the body with femininity and the mind with masculinity" (1989, 194). How some bodies came to be viewed as "more bodily" than others is a puzzle that Ruddick answers by arguing that the lack of intellectual control over menstruation, pregnancy, labor, and nursing set such female bodily functions against reason, which was viewed as detached, controlled, and impersonal—that is, masculine.

Even Simone de Beauvoir, while arguing that "one is not born, but rather becomes, a woman" (1953, 301), views childbirth and nursing as completely passive, and thus dehumanizing, processes, which keep women mired in immanence. She suggests that "it is not in giving life but in risking life that man is raised above the animal; that is why superiority has been accorded in humanity not to the sex that brings forth but to that which kills" (1953, 72). Although Beauvoir rejects the conclusion that this sex difference justifies male dominance, she nonetheless accepts the premise reducing childbirth to a purely "animal" function.[20]

Beauvoir was the first female philosopher I read and, as a teenager, I shared her disdain for (socially) compulsory marriage and maternity for women in this society. I still share her concerns about constraints on women's reproductive freedom, but I reject her view of pregnancy and motherhood as necessarily passive and tedious processes, even when voluntary. The work of Ruddick and other feminists who have been redefining motherhood has led me to see the liberatory potential in *chosen* maternity, childbirth, and childrearing. Reading Ruddick's *Maternal Thinking* in 1989, I recognized the ways in which my philosophical training had exacerbated my preexisting tendency to value the cerebral over the corporeal. In pursuing the life of the mind, I had accepted unthinkingly (because unconsciously) its incompatibility with the life of the (gestating and birthing) female body. My reading of Ruddick happened to coincide with a visit to a gynecologist who told me that I might have difficulty conceiving and that if I even suspected I would want to have a child someday I should start trying now. My philosophical bias against maternity, combined with a personal (and political) reaction against what I perceived as pressure to have a baby (as in the words of one academic woman's mother who said, "I'd rather be a grandmother than the mother of a Ph.D.") suddenly gave way to the startling realization that I might *want* to experience the particular kind of embodiment and connection pregnancy and motherhood provide, and that these things were not incompatible with being a philosopher. After years of considering my body little more than an unruly nuisance, I found myself wanting to yield up control over it, to learn what it had to teach me, to experience the abandon of labor and childbirth, what Margaret Walker has called "the willing or grateful surrender of 'I' to flesh."[21]

Plato praised those "who long to beget spiritually, not physically, the progeny which it is the nature of the soul to create and bring to birth. If you ask what that progeny is, it is wisdom and virtue in general. . . . Everyone would prefer children such as these to children after the flesh" (quoted in Ruddick 1989, 192–193). It occurred to me that this preference was not, after all, universal, and that, in any case, one did not have to choose between pursuing wisdom and virtue, on the one hand, and having children, on the other. My husband (who never felt as compelled to make such a choice) and I started trying to conceive, or, rather, as a friend put it more aptly, stopped trying not to. It was just six months later, however, that I was jumped from behind, beaten, raped, strangled, and left for dead in a ravine. The pleasures of embodiment were suddenly replaced by the pain and terror to which being embodied makes one prey.

I was no longer the same person I had been before the assault, and one of the ways in which I seemed changed was that I had a different relationship with my body. My body was now perceived as an enemy, having betrayed my new-found trust and interest in it, and as a site of increased vulnerability. But rejecting the body and returning to the life of the mind was not an option, since body and mind had become nearly indistinguishable. My mental state (typically, depression) felt physiological, like lead in my veins, while my physical state (frequently, incapacitation by fear and anxiety) was the incarnation of a cognitive and emotional paralysis resulting from shattered assumptions about my safety in the world. The symptoms of PTSD gave the lie to a latent dualism that still informs society's most prevalent attitude to trauma, namely, that victims should buck up, put the past behind them, and get on with their lives. My hypervigilance, heightened startle response, insomnia, and other PTSD symptoms were no more psychological, if that is taken to mean under my conscious control, than were my heartrate and blood pressure.[22]

The intermingling of mind and body is also apparent in traumatic memories that remain in the body, in each of the senses, in the heart that races and skin that crawls whenever something resurrects the only slightly buried terror. As Jonathan Shay writes in his study of combat trauma, "Traumatic memory is not narrative. Rather, it is experience that reoccurs, either as full sensory replay of traumatic events in dreams or flashbacks, with all things seen, heard, smelled, and felt intact, or as disconnected fragments. These fragments may be inexplicable rage, terror, uncontrollable crying, or disconnected body states and sensations" (1994, 172). The main change in the modality as well as in the content of the most salient traumatic memories is that they are more tied to the body than memories are typically considered to be.

Sensory flashbacks are not, of course, merely a clinical phenomenon, nor are they peculiar to trauma. Proust describes the pleasantly vivid flashbacks brought on by the leisurely savoring of a tea-soaked madeleine (1981, 1:48–49).[23] Trauma, however, changes the nature and frequency of sensory, emotional, and physiological flashbacks. They are reminiscent of the traumatic event itself, as Shay writes, in that "[o]nce experiencing is under way, the survivor lacks authority to stop it or put it away. The helplessness associated with the original experience is replayed in the apparent helplessness to end or modify the reexperience once it has begun" (1994, 174). Traumatic flashbacks immobilize the body by rendering the will as useless as it is in a nightmare in which one desperately tries to flee, but remains frozen.

The bodily nature of traumatic memory complicates a standard philosophical quandary concerning which of two criteria of identity—continuous body or continuous memories—should be used to determine personal identity over time. Locke's bodily transfer puzzle in which we are asked to decide who survives "should the soul of a prince . . . enter and inform the body of a cobbler" (1974, 116) no longer presents us with an either/or choice, depending on which criterion we invoke. If memories are lodged in the body, the Lockean distinction between the memory criterion and that of bodily identity no longer applies.[24]

The study of trauma also replaces the traditional philosophical puzzle about whether the soul can survive the death of the body with the question of whether the self can reconstitute itself after obliteration at the hands of another, after what Cathy Winkler has labeled "social murder" (1991). Winkler describes the way in which, during a rape, the victim is defined out of existence by the attitudes and actions of the rapist, which incapacitate the victim's self. "Without our abilities to think and feel as we choose . . . our existence becomes like a body on life support," Winkler writes. "During an attack, victims have confronted social death, and grappled with it to save themselves" (1991, 14). The victim's inability to be—and to assert—her self in the context of a rape constitutes at least a temporary social death, one from which a self can be resurrected only with great difficulty and with the help of others.

In the aftermath of trauma, not only is the victim's bodily awareness changed,[25] but she may also attempt to change her body itself in an effort to enhance her control over it. Eating disorders are a common reaction to sexual abuse, as is dressing in ways that disguise one's body. After my own assault, I wished I could add eyes in the back of my head, but I settled for cutting my hair so short that, when viewed from behind, I might be mistaken for a man.

The study of trauma does not lead to the conclusion that the self can be identified with the body, but it does show how the body and one's perception of it are nonetheless essential components of the self. It also reveals the ways in which one's ability to feel at home in the world is as much a physical as an epistemological accomplishment. Jean Améry writes, of the person who is tortured, that from the moment of the first blow he loses "trust in the world," which includes "the irrational and logically unjustifiable belief in absolute causality perhaps, or the likewise blind belief in the validity of the inductive inference." More important, according to Améry, is the loss of the certainty that other persons "will respect my physical, and with it also my metaphysical, being. The boundaries of my body are also the boundaries of my self. My skin surface shields me against the external world. If I am to have trust, I must feel on it only what I *want* to feel. At the first blow, however, this trust in the world breaks down" (1995, 126). Améry goes on to compare torture to rape, an apt comparison, not only because both objectify and traumatize the victim, but also because the pain they inflict reduces the victim to flesh, to the purely physical. This reduction has a particularly anguished quality for female victims of sexual violence who are already viewed as more tied to nature than men and are sometimes treated as mere flesh.[26] It is as if the tormentor says with his blows, "You are nothing but a body, a mere object for my will—here, I'll prove it!"

Those who endure long periods of repeated torture often find ways of dissociating themselves from their bodies, that part of themselves which undergoes the torture. As the research of Herman (1992) and Terr (1994) has shown, child victims of sexual and other physical abuse often utilize this defense against annihilation of the self, and, in extreme cases, even develop multiple personalities that enable one or more "selves" to emerge unscathed from the abuse. Some adult victims of rape report a kind of splitting from their bodies during the assault, as well as a separation from their former selves in the aftermath of the rape.

Charlotte Delbo writes of her return from Auschwitz:

life was returned to me
and I am here in front of life
as though facing a dress
I cannot wear.
    (1995, 240)

A number of Holocaust survivors, whose former selves were virtually annihilated in the death camps, gave themselves new names after the war, Jean Améry (formerly Hans Maier) and Paul Celan (formerly Paul Antschel) being among the most well-known. In a startling reappropriation of the name (literally) imposed on him during his incarceration at Auschwitz, one survivor retained and published under the name "Ka-Tzetnik 135633," meaning "concentration camp inmate number 135633."[27] Others were forced to assume new names and national and religious identities (or, rather, the appearance of them) in order to avoid capture, and probable death, during the war. The dislocations suffered by what Rosi Braidotti has called "nomadic subjects" (1994) can be agonizing even when the migrations are voluntary or, as in the case of Eva Hoffman (1989), whose family moved from Poland to Canada when she was 13, involuntary, but unmarked by violence. Given how traumatic such relocations can be, it is almost unimaginable how people can survive self-disintegrating torture and then manage to rebuild themselves in a new country, a new culture, and a new language. Nermina Zildzo, a recent refugee from the war in Bosnia, describes her new life in America, in which she struggles to become someone who can be herself in English, as that of "a cadaver," which is to say, not a life at all.[28]

Some who survived the Holocaust, such as Delbo, have written about a distinct self that emerged in the camps and then, in some sense, stayed there after the liberation. "Auschwitz is so deeply etched in my memory that I cannot forget one moment of it.—So you are living with Auschwitz?—No. I live next to it," Delbo writes (1985, 2). "No doubt, I am very fortunate in not recognizing myself in the self that was in Auschwitz. To return from there was so improbable that it seems to me I was never there at all. . . . I live within a twofold being. The Auschwitz double doesn't bother me, doesn't interfere with my life. As though it weren't I at all. Without this split I would not have been able to revive" (1985, 3).

What can we conclude from these clinical studies and personal narratives of trauma concerning the relationship of one's self to one's body? Does trauma make one feel more or less tied to one's body? That may depend on one's ability to dissociate. Since I, like most victims of one-time traumatic events, did not dissociate during the assault, I felt (and continue to feel) more tied to my body than before, or, at any rate, more vulnerable to self-annihilation because of it.[29] Those who survived ongoing trauma by dissociating from their bodies may feel that an essential part of themselves was untouched by the trauma, but even they experience, in the aftermath, the physical intrusions of visceral traumatic memories.

These various responses to trauma—dissociation from one's body, separation from the self one was either before or during the trauma—have in common the attempt to distance one's (real) self from the bodily self that is being degraded, and whose survival demands that one do, or at any rate be subjected to, degrading things. But such an attempt is never wholly successful and the survivor's bodily sense of self is permanently altered by an encounter with death that leaves one feeling "marked" for life. The intense awareness of embodiment experienced by trauma survivors is not "the willing or grateful surrender of 'I' to flesh" described by Walker, but more akin to the pain of Kafka's "harrow," cutting the condemned man's "sentence" deeper and deeper into his body until it destroys him.[30]

The Self as Narrative

Locke famously identified the self with a set of continuous memories, a kind of ongoing narrative of one's past that is extended with each new experience (1974). The study of trauma presents a fatal challenge to this view, since memory is so drastically disrupted by traumatic events, unless one is prepared to accept the conclusion that survivors of such events are distinct from their former selves. The literature on trauma does seem to support the view, advocated by Derek Parfit (1986), that the unitary self is an illusion and that we are all composed of a series of successive selves.[31] But how does one remake a self from the scattered shards of disrupted memory? Delbo writes of memories being stripped away from the inmates of the death camps, and of the incomprehensibly difficult task of getting them back after the war: "The survivor must undertake to regain his memory, regain what he possessed before: his knowledge, his experience, his childhood memories, his manual dexterity and his intellectual faculties, sensitivity, the capacity to dream, imagine, laugh" (1995, 255).

This passage illustrates a major obstacle to the trauma survivor's reconstructing a self in the sense of a remembered and ongoing narrative about oneself. Not only are one's memories of an earlier life lost, along with the ability to envision a future, but one's basic cognitive and emotional capacities are gone, or radically altered, as well. This epistemological crisis leaves the survivor with virtually no bearings to navigate by. As Améry writes, "Whoever has succumbed to torture can no longer feel at home in the world" (1995, 136). Shattered assumptions about the world and one's safety in it can, to some extent, eventually be pieced back together, but this is a slow and painful process. Although the survivor recognizes, at some level, that these regained assumptions are illusory, she learns that they are necessary illusions, as unshakable, ultimately, as cognitively impenetrable perceptual illusions.[32]

In addition, though, trauma can obliterate one's former emotional repertoire, leaving only a kind of counterfactual, propositional knowledge of emotions. When alerted to the rumors that the camp in which he was incarcerated would be evacuated the next day, Primo Levi felt no emotion, just as for many months he had "no longer felt any pain, joy or fear" except in a conditional manner: "if I still had my former sensitivity, I thought, this would be an extremely moving moment" (1993, 152–153). The inability to feel one's former emotions, even in the aftermath of trauma, leaves the survivor not only numbed, but also without the motivation to carry out the task of constructing an ongoing narrative.

Some have suggested that an additional reason why trauma survivors are frequently unable to construct narratives to make sense of themselves and to convey what they experienced is that, as Levi writes, "our language lacks words to express this offense, the demolition of a man" (1985, 9). It is debatable, however, whether that is the case, or whether the problem is simply others' refusal to hear survivors' stories, which makes it difficult for survivors to tell them even to themselves. As Paul Fussell observes, in his account of World War I:

> One of the cruxes of war . . . is the collision
> between events and the language available—or
> thought appropriate—to describe them. . . .

Logically, there is no reason why the English
language could not perfectly well render the
actuality of . . . warfare: it is rich in terms like
*blood, terror, agony, madness, shit, cruelty, murder,
sell-out* and *hoax*, as well as phrases like *legs blown
off, intestines gushing out over his hands, screaming
all night, bleeding to death from the rectum*, and the
like. . . . The problem was less one of "language"
than of gentility and optimism. . . . What listener
wants to be torn and shaken when he doesn't have
to be? We have made *unspeakable* mean
indescribable: it really means *nasty.* (1975, 169–170)

In order to construct self-narratives we need not only the
words with which to tell our stories, but also an audience
able and willing to hear us and to understand our words as
we intend them. This aspect of remaking a self in the aftermath of trauma highlights the dependency of the self on
others and helps to explain why it is so difficult for survivors
to recover when others are unwilling to listen to what they
endured.

Survivors attempting to construct narratives out of their
traumatic memories also encounter the obstacle of despair,
of the seeming futility of using language to change the world
and the pointlessness of doing anything else. Commenting
on the inability of language to convey the horror of what he
witnessed in the Warsaw ghetto, Abraham Lewin writes:

Perhaps because the disaster is so great there is
nothing to be gained by expressing in words
everything that we feel. Only if we were capable of
tearing out by the force of our pent-up anguish the
greatest of all mountains, a Mount Everest, and with
all our hatred and strength hurling it down on the
heads of the German murderers of our young and
old—this would be the only fitting reaction on our
part. Words are beyond us now. Our hearts are
empty and made of stone. (May 25, 1942; quoted in
Langer 1995a, 3)

As Langer comments, it is not "the poverty of language" Lewin rebukes in this passage, but, rather, its uselessness "as a weapon against the current enemy bent on destroying him and his fellow victims" (1995a, 3). Lewin was writing this during the war, however, and one might think that this explanation would not apply to those constructing narratives out of memory from a position of relative safety and power after the war. Granted, bearing witness makes more sense, and even comes to seem imperative, once one is able to be heard by those willing to help. It can be difficult, though, for survivors to realize when this occurs, and to tell their stories when it does, due to the obliteration of their sense of time. Primo Levi describes the disappearance of the future in the minds of the prisoners in Auschwitz:

> Memory is a curious instrument: ever since I have been in the camp, two lines written by a friend of mine a long time ago have been running through my mind:
> '. . . Until one day
> there will be no more sense in saying: tomorrow.'
> It is like that here. Do you know how one says 'never' in camp slang? '*Morgen früh*', tomorrow morning (1993, 133).

According to John Rawls, the possession of a "rational plan of life" (1971, 561) is essential to personhood, or, at any rate, to moral personhood. Diana Meyers argues that this ability to envisage, pursue, and carry out one's rational plan of life is a prerequisite for self-respect (1986). But the ability to form a plan of life is lost when one loses a sense of one's temporal being, as happened to Levi and the other prisoners in Auschwitz: "We had not only forgotten our country and our culture, but also our family, our past, the future we had imagined for ourselves, because, like animals, we were confined to the present moment" (1989, 75). Thinking of his former life, Levi noted, "Today the only thing left of the life of those days is what one needs to suffer hunger and cold; I am not even alive enough to know how to kill myself" (1989, 143–144).

The disappearance of the past and the foreshortening of the future are common symptoms among those who have survived long-lasting trauma of various kinds. As Jonathan Shay observes in his study of combat trauma in Vietnam War veterans, "The destruction of time is an inner survival skill. These words, written about concentration camp prisoners, apply equally to soldiers in prolonged combat:

> Thinking of the future stirs up such intense yearning and hope that . . . it [is] unbearable; they quickly learn that these emotions . . . will make them desperate. . . . The future is reduced to a matter of hours or days. Alterations in time sense begin with the obliteration of the future but eventually progress to obliteration of the past. . . . Thus prisoners are eventually reduced to living in an endless present. (Shay 1994, 176, quoting Herman 1992, 89)

The shrinking of time to the immediate present is also experienced in the aftermath of trauma, at least until the traumatic episode is integrated into the survivor's life narrative. "My former life?" Delbo wrote after being returned to Paris from the death camps. "Had I had a former life? My life afterwards? Was I alive to have an afterwards, to know what afterwards meant? I was floating in a present devoid of reality" (1995, 237). The unreality of Delbo's experience resulted not only from the absence of a past and future, but also from the lack of connection with others who could understand what she had survived. Much of her writing about what she endured in the camps took the form of imagined conversations with others in her convoy (Delbo 1995, 233–354). Recreating this community of survivors who could bear witness to one another and know that they would be heard may have been a crucial part of Delbo's recovery.

By constructing and telling a narrative of the trauma endured, and with the help of understanding listeners, the

—

survivor begins not only to integrate the traumatic episode into a life with a before and an after, but also to gain control over the occurrence of intrusive memories. When I was hospitalized after my assault I experienced moments of reprieve from vivid and terrifying flashbacks when giving my account of what had happened—to the police, doctors, a psychiatrist, a lawyer, and a prosecutor. Although others apologized for putting me through what seemed to them a retraumatizing ordeal, I responded that it was, even at that early stage, therapeutic to bear witness in the presence of others who heard and believed what I told them. Two and a half years later, when my assailant was brought to trial, I found it healing to give my testimony in public and to have it confirmed by the police, the prosecutor, my lawyer, and, ultimately, the jury, who found my assailant guilty of rape and attempted murder.[33]

How might we account for this process of "mastering the trauma" through repeated telling of one's story? The residue of trauma is a kind of body memory, as Roberta Culbertson notes, "full of fleeting images, the percussion of blows, sounds, and movements of the body—disconnected, cacophonous, the cells suffused with the active power of adrenalin, or coated with the anesthetizing numbness of noradrenalin" (1995, 174). Whereas traumatic memories (especially perceptual and emotional flashbacks) feel as though they are passively endured, narratives are the result of certain obvious choices (e.g., how much to tell to whom, in what order, etc.). This is not to say that the narrator is not subject to the constraints of memory or that the story will ring true however it is told. And the telling itself may be out of control, compulsively repeated. But one can control certain aspects of the narrative and that control, repeatedly exercised, leads to greater control over the memories themselves, making them less intrusive and giving them the kind of meaning that enables them to be integrated into the rest of life.

Not only present listeners, but also one's cultural heritage, can determine to a large extent the way in which an event is remembered and retold, and may even lead one to respond as though one remembered what one did not in fact experience.[34] Yael Tamir, an Israeli philosopher, told me a story illustrating cultural memory, in which she and her husband, neither of whom had been victims or had family members who had been victims of the Holocaust, literally jumped at the sound of a German voice shouting instructions at a train station in Switzerland. The experience triggered such vivid "memories" of the deportation that they grabbed their suitcases and fled the station. Marianne Hirsch (1992–93) discusses the phenomenon of "postmemory" in children of Holocaust survivors and Tom Segev writes of the ways in which the Holocaust continues to shape Israeli identity: "Just as the Holocaust imposed a posthumous collective identity on its six million victims, so too it formed the collective identity of this new country—not just for the survivors who came after the war but for all Israelis, then and now" (1993, 11). The influence of cultural memory on all of us is additional evidence of the deeply relational nature of the narrative self.

The relational nature of the self is also revealed by a further obstacle confronting trauma survivors attempting to reconstruct coherent narratives: the difficulty of regaining one's voice, one's subjectivity, after one has been reduced to silence, to the status of an object, or, worse, made into someone else's speech, an instrument of another's agency. Those entering Nazi concentration camps had the speech of their captors literally inscribed on their bodies. As Levi describes it, the message conveyed by the prisoners' tattoos was "You no longer have a name; this is your new name." It was "a non-verbal message, so that the innocent would feel his sentence written on his flesh" (1989, 119).[35]

One of the most chilling stories of a victim's body being used as another's speech is found in the biblical story of the traveling Levite, a story that also reveals the extent of our cultural complicity in the refusal to see trauma from the victim's perspective. The Levite's host had been approached at his home by members of a hostile tribe who asked him to hand over the Levite, so that they could rape him. This the host refused to do: instead, he offered to the angry crowd the Levite's wife, who was then, with the clear complicity of the Levite, shoved out the door. The Levite's wife (who is unnamed in the Bible, but is given the name "Beth" by Mieke Bal in her account of this story) was gang-raped all night, and when the Levite found her body in the morning (whether she was alive or dead is not clarified in the text) he put her on a donkey, took her home, and cut up her body into twelve pieces, which were then sent as messages to the tribes of Israel.[36]

This biblical story is a striking example of a woman's body used as men's language. (Other instances include rape as the humiliation of the man whose "property" is stolen or as a nation's sign of victory in war, as well as some forms of pornography.) Reflecting on this story reveals some parallels between the dismemberment and dispersal of Beth and the shattered self and fractured speech of the survivor of trauma. Piecing together a dismembered self seems to require a process of remembering in which speech and affect converge. This working through, or remastering of, the traumatic memory involves going from being the medium of someone else's (the torturer's) speech to being the subject of one's own. The results of the process of working through reveal the performative role of speech acts in recovering from trauma: *saying* something about a traumatic memory *does* something to it. As Shay notes in the case of Vietnam veterans, "Severe trauma explodes the cohesion of consciousness. When a survivor creates fully realized narrative that brings together the shattered knowledge of what happened, the emotions that were aroused by the meanings of the events, and the bodily sensations that the physical events created, the survivor pieces back together the fragmentation of consciousness that trauma has caused" (1994, 188). But one cannot recover in isolation, since "[n]arrative heals personality changes only if the survivor finds or creates a trustworthy community of listeners for it" (1994, 188). As Levi observes, "Part of our existence lies in the feelings of those near to us. This is why the experience of someone who has lived for days during which man was merely a thing in the eyes of man is non-human" (1993, 172). Fortunately, just as one can be reduced to an object through torture, one can become a human subject again through telling one's narrative to caring others who are able to listen.

Intense psychological pressures make it difficult, however, for others to listen to trauma narratives. Cultural repression of traumatic memories (in the United States about slavery, in Germany and Poland and elsewhere about the Holocaust) comes not only from an absence of empathy with victims, but also out of an active fear of empathizing with those whose terrifying fate forces us to acknowledge that we are not in control of our own. I recently felt my own need to distance myself from a survivor's trauma when I read the story of Ruth Elias, who was three months pregnant when she arrived in Auschwitz in December 1943. After she gave birth, Josef Mengele decided to experiment on her son to see how long a newborn could live without food. "In the beginning, the baby was crying all the time," Elias recalled. "Then only whimpering." After a week, a Jewish doctor took pity on her and gave her some morphine with which she euthanized her child. "It didn't take long before the child stopped breathing. . . . I didn't want to live anymore."[37] How she managed (how she manages) to continue living is incomprehensible to me. I realize, though, that I manage to bear the knowledge of such an atrocity by denying that such a thing could ever happen to a child of mine. I can (now) live with the (vivid) possibility that I might be murdered. But I cannot live with even the possibility that this kind of torture could be inflicted on my child. So I employ the usual defenses: it couldn't happen here/now/to me/and so on.

As a society, we live with the unbearable by pressuring those who have been traumatized to forget and by rejecting the testimonies of those who are forced by fate to remember. As individuals and as cultures, we impose arbitrary term limits on memory and on recovery from trauma: a century, say, for slavery, fifty years, perhaps, for the Holocaust, a decade or two for Vietnam, several months for mass rape or serial murder. Even a public memorialization can be a forgetting, a way of saying to survivors what someone said after I published my first article on sexual violence: "Now you can put this behind you." But attempting to limit traumatic memories does not make them go away; the signs and symptoms of trauma remain, caused by a source more virulent for being driven underground.

In *The Book of Laughter and Forgetting*, Milan Kundera writes that "The struggle against power is the struggle of memory against forgetting."[38] Whether the power is a fascist state or an internalized trauma, surviving the present requires the courage to confront the past, reexamine it, retell it, and thereby remaster its traumatic aspects. As Eva Hoffman, who returns repeatedly in her memoir to a past in which she was "lost in translation" after moving from Poland to Canada, explains, "Those who don't understand the past may be condemned to repeat it, but those who never repeat it are condemned not to understand it" (1989, 278).

And so we repeat our stories, and we listen to others'. What Hoffman writes of her conversations with Miriam, her closest North American friend, could also describe the remaking of a survivor's self in relation to empathic others: "To a large extent, we're the keepers of each other's stories, and the shape of these stories has unfolded in part from our interwoven accounts. Human beings don't only search for meanings, they are themselves units of meaning; but we can mean something only within the fabric of larger significations" (1989, 279). Trauma, however, unravels whatever meaning we've found and woven ourselves into, and so listening to survivors' stories is, as Lawrence Langer describes reading and writing about the Holocaust, "an experience in *un*learning; both parties are forced into the Dantean gesture of abandoning all safe props as they enter and, without benefit of Virgil, make their uneasy way through its vague domain" (1995b, 6–7). It is easy to understand why one would not willingly enter such a realm, but survivors' testimonies must be heard, if individual and cultural recovery is to be possible.

To recover from trauma, according to psychoanalyst

Dori Laub, a survivor needs to construct a narrative and tell it to an empathic listener, in order to reexternalize the event. "Bearing witness to a trauma is, in fact, a process that includes the listener" (1992, 70). And to the extent that bearing witness reestablishes the survivor's identity, the empathic other is essential to the continuation of a self. Laub writes of Chaim Guri's film, *The Eighty-First Blow*, which "portrays the image of a man who narrates the story of his sufferings in the camps only to hear his audience say: 'All this cannot be true, it could not have happened. You must have made it up.' This denial by the listener inflicts, according to the film, the ultimately fateful blow, beyond the eighty blows that man, in Jewish tradition, can sustain and survive" (1992, 68).

The Autonomous Self

The view of the self most central to ethics, as well as to social, political, and legal philosophy (at least in the analytic tradition), is one that holds that the self is the locus of autonomous agency, that which freely makes choices and wills actions. This is a self that is considered responsible for its decisions and actions and is an appropriate subject of praise or blame. It is the transformation of the self as autonomous agent that is perhaps most apparent in survivors of trauma. First, the autonomy-undermining symptoms of PTSD reconfigure the survivor's will, rendering involuntary many responses that were once under voluntary control. Intrusive memories are triggered by things reminiscent of the traumatic event and carry a strong, sometimes overwhelming, emotional charge. Not only is one's response to items that would startle anyone heightened, but one has an involuntary startle response to things that formerly provoked no reaction or a subtler, still voluntary one. The loss of control evidenced by these and other PTSD symptoms alters who one is, not only in that it limits what one can do (and can refrain from doing), but also in that it changes what one *wants* to do.

A trauma survivor suffers a loss of control not only over herself, but also over her environment, and this, in turn, can lead to a constriction of the boundaries of her will. If a rape victim is unable to walk outside without the fear of being assaulted again, she quickly loses the desire to go for a walk. If one's self, or one's *true* self, is considered to be identical with one's will, then a survivor cannot be considered to be the same as her pre-trauma self, since what she is able to will post-trauma is so drastically altered. Some reactions that once were under the will's command become involuntary and some desires that once were motivating can no longer be felt, let alone acted upon.

Such loss of control over oneself can explain, to a large extent, what a survivor means in saying, "I am no longer myself." The trauma survivor identifies with her former self not only because that self was more familiar and less damaged, but also because it was more predictable. The fact that, as has been recently discovered, certain drugs, such as Prozac, give PTSD sufferers greater self-control, by making them better able to choose their reactions to things and the timing of their responses, accounts for the common response to such drugs: "they make me more myself" (Kramer 1993). It may also be that after taking Prozac such a person is better able to endorse, or identify with, her new self.[39]

In order to recover, a trauma survivor needs to be able to control herself, control her environment (within reasonable limits), and be reconnected with humanity. Whether the latter two achievements occur depends, to a large extent, on other people. Living with the memory of trauma is living with a kind of disability, and whether one is able to function with a disability depends largely on how one's social and physical environments are set up (Minow 1990). A trauma survivor makes accommodations, figuring out how to live with her limits, but she also realizes that at least some externally imposed limits can be changed. In the year after my assault, when I was terrified to walk alone, I was able to go to talks and other events on campus by having a friend walk with me. I became able to use the locker room in the gym after getting the university to put a lock on a door that led to a dark, isolated passageway, and I was able to park my car at night after lobbying the university to put a light in the parking lot.

These ways of enhancing my autonomy in the aftermath of my assault reinforced my view of autonomy as fundamentally dependent on others. Not only is autonomy compatible with socialization and with caring for and being cared for by others (Meyers 1987, 1989, 1992), but the right sort of interactions with others can be seen to be essential to autonomy. In "Jurisprudence and Gender," Robin West (1988) discusses the tension within feminist theory between, on the one hand, the desire for connection and fear of alienation (in cultural feminism)[40] and, on the other hand, the desire for autonomy and fear of invasion (in radical or "dominance" feminism).[41] Once one acknowledges the relational nature of autonomy, however, this apparent tension can be resolved by noting that the main reason all of us, especially women, have to fear violent intrusions by others is that they severely impair our ability to be connected to humanity in ways we value. It is this loss of connection that trauma survivors mourn, a loss that in turn imperils autonomous selfhood. In order to reestablish that connection in the aftermath of trauma, one must first feel able to protect oneself against invasion. The autonomous self and the relational self are thus shown to be interdependent, even constitutive of one another.

Virginia Held defends a relational account of autonomy in which autonomy does not consist of putting walls around oneself or one's property (as in Isaiah Berlin's phrase for autonomy, "the inner citadel"),[42] but instead, of forming essential relationships with others. Held cites Jennifer Nedelsky, who suggests that "the most promising model, symbol, or metaphor for autonomy is not property, but childrearing. There we have encapsulated the emergence of autonomy through relationship with others. . . . Interdependence [is] a constant component of autonomy" (Nedelsky 1989, 11).

Trauma survivors are dependent on empathic others who are willing to listen to their narratives. Given that the language in which such narratives are conveyed and are understood is itself a social phenomenon, this aspect of recovery from trauma also underscores the extent to which autonomy is a fundamentally relational notion.[43]

Primo Levi recalls a dream in which he is telling his sister and others about the camp and they are completely indifferent, acting as though he is not there. Many others in the camp had this dream. "Why does it happen?" he asks. "Why is the pain of every day translated so constantly into our dreams, in the ever-repeated scene of the unlistened-to story?" (1993, 60). Why is it so horrifying for survivors to be unheard? There is a scene in the film *La Famiglia* (Ettore Scola, 1987) in which a little boy's uncle pretends not to see him, a game that quickly turns from a bit of fun into a kind of torture when the man persists long beyond the boy's tolerance for invisibility. For the child, not to be seen is not to exist, to be annihilated. Not to be heard means that the self the survivor has become does not exist for these others. Since the earlier self died, the surviving self needs to be known and acknowledged in order to exist.

This illuminates a connection among the views of the self as narrative, as embodied, and as autonomous. It is not sufficient for mastering the trauma to construct a narrative of it: one must (physically, publicly) say or write (or paint or film) the narrative and others must see or hear it in order for one's survival as an autonomous self to be complete. This reveals the extent to which the self is created and sustained by others and, thus, is able to be destroyed by them. The boundaries of the will are limited, or enlarged, not only by the stories others tell, but also by the extent of their ability and willingness to listen to ours.

In the traditional philosophical literature on personal identity, one is considered to be the same person over time if one can (now) identify with that person in the past or future. One typically identifies with a person in the past if one can remember having that person's experiences and one identifies with a person in the future if one cares in a unique way about that person's future experiences. An interesting result of group therapy with trauma survivors is that they come to have greater compassion for their earlier selves by empathizing with others who experienced similar traumas. They stop blaming themselves by realizing that others who acted or reacted similarly are not blameworthy. Rape survivors, who typically have difficulty getting angry with their assailants, find that in group therapy they are able to get angry on their own behalf by first getting angry on behalf of others (Koss and Harvey 1991).

That survivors gain the ability to reconnect with their former selves by empathizing with others who have experienced similar traumas reveals the extent to which we exist only in connection with others. It also suggests that healing from trauma takes place by a kind of splitting off of the traumatized self which one then is able to empathize with, just as one empathizes with others.[44] The loss of a trauma survivor's former self is typically described by analogy to the loss of a beloved other. And yet, in grieving for another, one often says, "It's as though a part of myself has died." It is not clear whether this circular comparison is a case of language failing us or, on the contrary, its revealing a deep truth about selfhood and connectedness. By finding (some aspects of) one's lost self in another person, one can manage (to a greater or lesser degree) to reconnect with it and to reintegrate one's various selves into a coherent personality.

The fundamentally relational character of the self is also highlighted by the dependence of survivors on others' attitudes toward them in the aftermath of trauma. Victims of rape and other forms of torture often report drastically altered senses of self-worth, resulting from their degrading treatment. That even one person—one's assailant—treated one as worthless can, at least temporarily, undo an entire lifetime of self-esteem (see Roberts 1989, 91). This effect is magnified by prolonged exposure to degradation, in a social and historical context in which the group to which one belongs is despised. Survivors of trauma recover to a greater or lesser extent depending on others' responses to them after the trauma. These aspects of trauma and recovery reveal the deeply social nature of one's sense of self and underscore the limits of the individual's capacity to control her own self-definition.

But what can others do to help a survivor recover from trauma, apart from listening empathically? Kenneth Seeskin argues, in discussing an appropriate response to the Holocaust, that we who did not experience it cannot hope to understand it and yet to remain silent in the aftermath of it would be immoral. And so, he suggests, we should move beyond theory, beyond an attempt to understand it, to a practice of resistance. As Emil Fackenheim writes, "The truth is that to grasp the Holocaust whole-of-horror is not to comprehend or transcend it, but rather *to say no to it, or resist it.*"[45] The "no" of resistance is not the "no" of denial. It is the "no" of acknowledgment of what happened and refusal to let it happen again.

Remaking Oneself

A child gave me a flower
one morning
a flower picked
for me
he kissed the flower
before giving it to me. . . .
There is no wound that will not heal
I told myself that day
and still repeat it from time to time
but not enough to believe it.
—Charlotte Delbo (1995, 241)

What is the goal of the survivor? Ultimately, it is not to transcend the trauma, not to solve the dilemmas of survival, but simply to endure. This can be hard enough, when the only way to regain control over one's life seems to be to end it. A few months after my assault, I drove by myself for several hours to visit a friend. Although driving felt like a much safer mode of transportation than walking, I worried throughout the journey, not only about the trajectory of every oncoming vehicle, but also about my car breaking down, leaving me at the mercy of potentially murderous passers-by. I wished I'd had a gun so that I could shoot myself rather than be forced to live through another assault.[46] Later in my recovery, as depression gave way to rage, such suicidal thoughts were quickly quelled by a stubborn refusal to finish my assailant's job for him. I also learned, after martial arts training, that I was capable, morally as well as physically, of killing in self-defense—an option that made the possibility of another life-threatening attack one I could live with. Some rape survivors have remarked on the sense of moral loss they experienced when they realized that they could kill their assailants (and even wanted to!) but I think that this thought can be seen as a salutary character change in those whom society does not encourage to value their own lives enough.[47] And, far from jeopardizing their connections with a community, this newfound ability to defend themselves, and to consider themselves worth fighting for, enables rape survivors to move among others, free of debilitating fears. It gave me the courage to bring a child into the world, in spite of the realization that doing so would, far from making me immortal, make me twice as mortal, by doubling my chances of having my life destroyed by a speeding truck.[48]

But many trauma survivors who endured much worse than I did, and for much longer, found, often years later, that it was impossible to go on. It is not a moral failing to leave a world that has become morally unacceptable. I wonder how some can ask, of battered women, "Why didn't they leave?" while saying, of those driven to suicide by the brutal and inescapable aftermath of trauma, "Why didn't they stay?" Améry wrote, "Whoever was tortured, stays tortured" (1995, 131) and this may explain why he, Levi, Celan, and other Holocaust survivors took their own lives decades after their (physical) torture ended, as if such an explanation were needed.

Those who have survived trauma understand well the pull of that solution to their daily Beckettian dilemma, "I can't go on, I must go on," for on some days the conclusion "I'll go on" cannot be reached by faith or reason.[49] How does one go on with a shattered self, with no guarantee of recovery, believing that one will always "stay tortured" and never "feel at home in the world"? One hopes for a bearable future, in spite of all the inductive evidence to the contrary. After all, the loss of faith in induction following an unpredictable trauma also has a reassuring side: since inferences from the past can no longer be relied upon to predict the future, there's no more reason to think that tomorrow will bring agony than to think that it won't. So one makes a wager, in which nothing is certain and the odds change daily, and sets about willing to believe that life, for all its unfathomable horror, still holds some undiscovered pleasures.[50] And one remakes oneself by finding meaning in a life of caring for and being sustained by others. While I used to have to will myself out of bed each day, I now wake gladly to feed my son whose birth, four years after the assault, gives me reason not to have died. He is the embodiment of my life's new narrative and I am more autonomous by virtue of being so intermingled with him. Having him has also enabled me to rebuild my trust in the world around us. He is so trusting that, before he learned to walk, he would stand with outstretched arms, wobbling, until he fell, stiff-limbed, forwards, backwards, certain the universe would catch him. So far, it has, and when I tell myself it always will, the part of me that he's become believes it.

Memory is an action: essentially it is the action of telling
a story.
—Pierre Janet[1]

Acts of Memory

CHAPTER   FOUR

Dori Laub quotes a Holocaust survivor who said, "We wanted to survive so as to live one day after Hitler, in order to be able to tell our story."[2] As Laub came to believe, after listening to many Holocaust testimonies and working as an analyst with survivors and their children, such victims of trauma "did not only need to survive in order to tell their story; they also needed to tell their story in order to survive."[3] Telling their story, narrating their experiences of traumatic events, has long been considered—at least since Freud and Janet[4]—to play a significant role in survivors' recovery from trauma. Despite many decades of clinical and theoretical work on the subject of trauma and narrative, *why* narratives play such an important role in surviving the aftermath of trauma remains somewhat of a mystery.

The undoing of the self in trauma involves a radical disruption of memory, a severing of past from present, and, typically, an inability to envision a future.[5] And yet trauma survivors often eventually find ways to reconstruct themselves and carry on with reconfigured lives. Working through, or remastering, traumatic memory (in the case of human-inflicted trauma) involves a shift from being the object or medium of someone else's (the perpetrator's) speech (or other expressive behavior) to being the subject of one's own. The act of bearing witness to the trauma facilitates this shift, not only by transforming traumatic memory into a narrative that can then be worked into the survivor's sense of self and view of the world, but also by reintegrating the survivor into a community, reestablishing connections essential to selfhood.

In this chapter, I examine some of the ways in which telling, writing, reading, and listening to first-person narratives can play a significant role in the remaking of a self. I also discuss the limits of narrative as a means to recovery. For some trauma survivors, talk therapy must be supplemented by action, for example, self-defense training—a kind of embodied narrative itself—or political action. And psychopharmacological intervention may be necessary in order to make psychic change physiologically possible.

Memories of traumatic events can be themselves traumatic—uncontrollable, intrusive, and frequently somatic. They
are experienced by the survivor as inflicted, not chosen—as
flashbacks to the events themselves. That they are experienced in this way does not, however, give them epistemo-
logically privileged status, as snapshots of how things "really
were." Some trauma theorists, for example, Caruth and van
der Kolk and van der Hart, seem to assume an identity
between involuntary, especially vivid, perceptions (flashbacks
and nightmares of traumatic experiences) and veridical (or
literal) ones.⁶ On their view, these three features allegedly go
together in traumatic memory: involuntariness (this may
include, or be highlighted by, repetitiveness), vividness (this
may include consistency over time), and veridicality ("literality" in Caruth and van der Kolk and van der Hart). It
seems as if the first two are taken as evidence for the third (à
la Descartes and Hume), since no independent evidence is
offered for it. But certain perceptual illusions ("cognitively
impenetrable" ones) cannot be willed away, and some illusions (those in lifelike dreams, for example) are at least as
vivid as many veridical perceptions.

Other features allegedly characterizing traumatic memories on this view are that: they are unpleasant (that is, they
are *of* states—and they induce states—we would rather
avoid), they are delayed (occurring, or at any rate capable of
occurring, long after the precipitating event), and they are
surprising, that is, they are remembrances of events that
were never experienced (in their entirety? with such vividness?) in the first place. But these features don't necessarily
(or even typically) appear along with the first three mentioned. The taste of Proust's madeleine, for example,
prompted a memory, indeed a whole host of memories, that
were unbidden, lifelike, delayed, and ostensibly veridical. But
they were also pleasant.⁷

Caruth and van der Kolk and van der Hart present it as

something of a paradox that in traumatic memory there is the conjunction of the elision of memory and the precision of recall. (Caruth traces this idea back to Freud; van der Kolk and van der Hart trace it back to Janet.) "Indeed," Caruth writes, "the literal registration of an event—the capacity to continually, in the flashback, reproduce it in exact detail—appears to be connected, in traumatic experience, precisely with the way it escapes full consciousness as it occurs. Modern neurobiologists have in fact suggested that the unerring 'engraving' on the mind, the 'etching into the brain' of an event in trauma may be associated with its elision of its normal encoding in memory" (Caruth 1995, 152–153).[8] Only the pathological memory, inacessible to consciousness, but active (and destructive) because of it, on this view, is true to the event, registering what really happened. It's accurate because untouched (like an unretouched photo), not worked over or thought about with the distorting categories of cognition. This apparently gives it privileged epistemological status as a bearer of the truth—as that which, for ethical and political reasons, must be preserved. This preservation, however, comes at the cost of ongoing pathology, and is in conflict with the survivor's goal of psychic recovery. "The danger of speech, of integration into the narration of memory, may lie not in what it cannot understand, but in that it understands too much," according to Caruth. "The possibility of integration into memory and the consciousness of history thus raises the question, van der Kolk and van der Hart ultimately observe, 'whether it is not a sacrilege of the traumatic experience to play with the reality of the past?'" (Caruth 1995, 154).

Such a theory of traumatic memory consigns the traumatized person to the status of credible (but—or because—sick) victim-witness *or* untrustworthy (but—or because—recovered) healthy survivor. This bind allegedly faced by the trauma survivor is uncomfortably reminiscent of the dilemma of the rape victim on the stand who is viewed as traumatized, because sick (emotional, hysterical), and, thus, not credible *or* as calm and reasonable, and thus clearly not traumatized, and so not credible. In a similar way, this theory of trauma makes it conceptually impossible for a survivor to bear reliable witness to the trauma. This is like saying that an eloquent art critic cannot possibly enhance our understanding of a painting because the symbol systems used in painting and in language are incommensurable. It's true that they're incommensurable. But it doesn't follow from this that silence before a painting is the only authentic (and ethically defensible) response.[9]

In contrast to the involuntary experiencing of traumatic memories, narrating memories to others (who are strong and empathic enough to be able to listen) enables survivors to gain more control over the traces left by trauma. Narrative memory is not passively endured; rather, it is an act on the part of the narrator, a speech act that defuses traumatic memory, giving shape and a temporal order to the events recalled, establishing more control over their recalling, and helping the survivor to remake a self.

In order to recover, a trauma survivor needs to be able to establish greater control over traumatic memories and other intrusive symptoms of PTSD, recover a sense of mastery over her environment (within reasonable limits), and be reconnected with humanity. Whether these achievements occur depends, as I have argued, on other people. By constructing and telling a narrative of the trauma endured, and with the help of understanding listeners, the survivor begins not only to integrate the traumatic episode into a life with a before and an after, but also to gain control over the occurrence of intrusive memories.

It is a curious feature of trauma narratives that, in the right circumstances, narrating a traumatic memory can help to defuse it. A useful (although not complete) analogy can be drawn between performative utterances as described by J. L. Austin and trauma testimonies. Performative utterances are defined by Austin, in part, as those in which "the uttering of the sentence is, or is a part of, the doing of an action, which . . . would not *normally* be described as, or as 'just', saying something (1962, 5)." In the case of trauma testimonies, the action could be described as transforming traumatic memory into narrative memory or as recovering or remaking the self. In the case of both performative utterances and trauma testimonies, cultural norms or conventions, as well as uptake on the part of some other individual(s), are required in order for the speech act to be successful (or, as Austin puts it, "felicitous").

There is also an important disanalogy, however, between performative utterances and trauma testimonies. According to Austin, performative utterances "do not 'describe' or 'report' or constate anything at all, are not 'true or false.'"[10] Trauma testimonies do purport to describe events that actually occurred. And what they *do*, or accomplish, if successful, is *un*do the effects of the very violence they describe.

Claims of memory—of the form "I remember that p"— are ambiguous. In one sense of "remembering" (which might more appropriately be called "seeming to remember"), such claims are about a present act of consciousness and can be true regardless of any correspondence to any past experience or state of affairs. In another sense of "remembering," one can correctly be said to remember only things that were once experienced. It may be that the performative, healing aspect of trauma testimonies is distinct from their functioning as reports of historical fact. That is, the same utterance could be (at least) two kinds of speech act: one of bearing witness (describing events as they occurred) and one of narrating or working through (and thus transforming) traumatic memories. The latter might have a performative aspect not shared by the former. One speech act might succeed, even if the other one does not. The description might succeed in describing the world as it was, even if the performative fails because of infelicitious conditions. Or vice versa.[11]

Although there are many varieties of trauma narrative, the form discussed most widely in the literature on trauma is that of a survivor telling her story to another person, often a therapist. Psychologists writing about trauma stress that one has to tell one's trauma narrative to an empathic *other* in order for the telling to be therapeutic. But some survivors are helped by telling their stories to *imagined* others—to potential readers, for example, or to others kept alive in a photograph.[12] Narrating a trauma involves externalizing it, but this can be done in a variety of ways. Simply writing in a journal can facilitate this, by temporarily splitting the self into an active—narrating—subject and a more passive—described—object. Even this can help to resubjectify a self objectified by trauma. It can also enable the survivor to gain greater empathy with herself. It was only when I managed to write a narrative of my assault, several months after the attack, and then *read* it, that I realized, "My God, what a horrible thing to happen to someone!"

Writing in others' imagined voices, as Charlotte Delbo has done in *Auschwitz and After*, can also be a way of externalizing and hearing, not only *their* narratives, but also the writer's own. Hearing *other* survivors' *actual* narratives, in the context of group therapy, can also be healing, in ways that go beyond the capacity of individual therapy. It can not only enable a survivor to feel empathy for her traumatized self (by first feeling it for another who experienced a similar trauma), but also make possible appropriate emotions, such as anger, that she was not able to feel on her own behalf. By first feeling empathy with other survivors and getting angry with *their* tormentors, she is better able to get angry with her own. Hearing others' narratives can also help trauma survivors to move beyond unjustified self-blame. (Well, if *she* clearly wasn't to blame for her assault, why should I blame myself for mine?)

One of the most serious harms of trauma is that of loss of control. Some researchers of trauma have defined it as a state of complete helplessness in the face of an overwhelming force.[13] Whether or not such total loss of control is constitutive of trauma, a daunting, seemingly impossible, task faced by the trauma survivor is to regain a sense of control over her or his life.[14] Trauma survivors (rape survivors, in particular, because they are frequently blamed for their assaults) are faced with an especially intractable double bind:

they need to know there's something they can do to avoid being similarly traumatized in the future, but if there *is* such a thing, then they blame themselves for not knowing it (or doing it) at the time. They are faced with a choice between regaining control by accepting (at least some) responsibility—and hence blame—for the trauma, or feeling overwhelmed by helplessness. Whereas rape victims' self-blaming has often been misunderstood as merely a self-destructive response to rape, arising out of low self-esteem, feelings of shame, or female masochism, and fueled by society's desire to blame the victim, it can also be seen as an adaptive survival strategy, if the victim has no other way of regaining a sense of control.[15]

The need for control reinforces, and is reinforced by, a fundamental assumption most of us share: our belief that we live in a just world, in which nothing that is both terrible and undeserved will happen to us.[16] Even though many of us recognize the delusory quality of such a belief, our desire to make sense of our experiences, including our random bad fortune, often swamps our better judgment. Social psychologists have observed that not only do others tend to blame and derogate victims of crime and disasters of various kinds, but victims tend to blame and disparage themselves even when it should be obvious that they could not have brought on their misfortune.[17]

One might think it would be easier, and it certainly would be more appropriate, for victims of violence to blame their assailants. But a further reason for the prevalence of self-blame among rape survivors, in addition to the need for control and the belief in a just world, is the difficulty so many of them have in getting angry with their assailants. I was stunned to discover that the other women in my rape survivors' support group were, like me, unable to feel anger toward their assailants, and I was surprised to learn later that this was not at all unusual. It was not until after I had taken a self-defense course that I was able to get angry with the man who had almost killed me.[18]

The difficulty of directing anger toward their attackers exacerbates trauma victims' tendency to blame themselves in order to feel more in control of their fate. Although self-blame can help victims regain a feeling of control, not all varieties of self-blame do. Psychologist Ronnie Janoff-Bulman (1979) has distinguished between behavioral self-blame, which attributes victimization to modifiable past behavior, and characterological self-blame, which attributes it to unalterable (and undesirable) character traits. She found that behavioral self-blame facilitates recovery by giving victims a sense of control, whereas characterological self-blame leaves victims feeling vulnerable and leads to a greater incidence of depression. This isn't surprising, since we tend to think that our behavior is under our control whereas our characters, to a large extent, are not. They are, on the contrary, what control us. Characterological self-blame also usually contributes to the loss of self-esteem already suffered by victims who have been subjected to degrading treatment by their assailants. The exception may be the case in which the victim is able to blame the assault on traits of a "former self" no longer possessed by a "current self."[19]

Behavioral self-blame, on the contrary, appears to lessen depression and facilitate recovery. Indeed, those victims who find themselves unable to engage in behavioral self-blame are left with feelings of extreme helplessness that can make recovery more difficult.[20] This helps to explain the observation that trauma survivors who did not anticipate the trauma (and thus could not have done anything to prevent it) have a more difficult time recovering, other things being equal, than those who saw what was coming and experienced anxiety ahead of time.[21] But even though behavioral self-blame can serve an adaptive function, it is a costly survival strategy for the victim, and it is not only fueled by, but also contributes to, society's erroneous and dangerous victim-blaming attitudes. Although this form of self-blame gives the victim the sense that she could avoid being assaulted again in the future by avoiding whatever "blameworthy" behavior "brought it on" in the past, it also leads to self-berating for her past "mistakes" and to unfair, and ultimately futile, self-imposed restrictions on her behavior.

But given that the alternative to self-blame appears to be feeling helpless, which is harder to bear, how can self-blame be avoided? One way for rape survivors, in particular, to break out of the double bind of self-blame or helplessness is, as I have argued, to take a self-defense course. Such training can, for some, usefully supplement talk therapy as a means of recovering from trauma. While learning self-defense does not guarantee that they will never be victimized again, it greatly increases their options for fending off assault,[22] and enables them to feel in control of their lives without having to blame themselves or to restrict their behavior in ways never expected of men. And, perhaps even more important, it makes it easier for victims to put the blame where it belongs: on their assailants. This is facilitated by the ability to feel appropriate anger toward them once the terror induced by helplessness subsides.[23]

Of course, self-defense instruction is not a panacea. It does not eliminate the problem of violence against women. It might even contribute to the common misperception of some types of trauma—rape, in particular—as individual rather than collective traumas. At best, it can give some people a greater chance of avoiding being victimized, most likely by deflecting the assailants' attention onto other targets.[24] I have been discussing here simply its role in helping a survivor to carry on in the aftermath of a violent assault.

The above discussion of self-defense training points to one limitation of purely linguistic narratives in enabling recovery from trauma. It may be that, in some cases, a kind of physical remastering of the trauma is necessary. In learning self-defense maneuvers and then imaginatively reenacting the traumatic event, in space as well as in the imagination, with the ability to change the ending, a survivor can gain even more control over traumatic memories. In recovering from trauma, a survivor may be helped not only by telling the story, but also by being able to rewrite the plot and then enact it.

Political activism (including lobbying for new legislation, speaking out, educating others, helping survivors) can also help to undo the double bind of self-blame versus helplessness. Some feminist critics of "the recovery movement" assume that concern for (or the quest for) the psychological well-being of individual survivors is somehow incompatible with (and drives out) political activism. For some survivors and activists, however, the two *must* go together.

On Meaning and Molecules

For me, narrative therapy, even when combined with self-defense training and political activism, was not enough to enable me to function, even marginally, in the wake of my assault. My physiological state—oscillating between hyper-vigilance and lethargy, between panic and despair—made political activism (or even getting out of bed some days) impossible. It's hard to see how I would have made it without pharmaceutical help. Unlike others—for example, Sharon Lamb (1999)—who consider the medical diagnoses of victims of sexual violence to be dismissive (and even destructive) of the survivor's agency, I felt enormous relief when I realized I had all the symptoms of PTSD and when I learned that there was evidence that it was a neurological condition, treatable by drugs. There's hope, I thought, it's chemical! After struggling for the first six months (after I left the hospital) to get better without medical assistance, it was liberating to think of myself as having a physical injury. This was similar to my relief when my sinus doctor said, in explaining my long history of chronic sinusitis, no, it's not that I'd been under too much stress, that I have a poor immune system, or—as an allergist actually told me—that I'd been duped by feminism into thinking I could have it all (career, kid, good health); it was, as he put it, "a purely mechanical problem." Not that this meant it—my condition—could necessarily be easily resolved (think of car problems!) but it did mean that it wasn't (entirely or exclusively) up to me to resolve it, that a third party with a certain expertise could intervene and set things right, that someone else might be, in fact, *better* situated than I was to make things (me) better.

Could my despair be a "purely mechanical problem"? Could I have faith in the power of drugs—a faith which, by itself, might heal me? It wasn't that simple. Prozac, which I started to take six months after my assault, brought me back to life. But I relapsed into debilitating depression periodically even while on antidepressants. The chemically enhanced communication among my neurotransmitters may have facilitated my getting out of bed in the morning, but it didn't tell me what to do next. It made things seem more do-able, but it didn't provide me with any reason for doing them. So, for me, medication was a necessary, but not a sufficient condition for recovery. What else was needed? A reconceptualization of the world and of my place in it. An actual world in which support and sustenance were available. A sense that my various images of the world—and the world itself—could someday coincide enough so that I could navigate my way around in it.

Over the past ten years I have tried more prescription drugs than I can now name. Various psychiatrists prescribed Prozac, Paxil, Zoloft, Effexor, Serzone, Wellbutrin, Ritalin—and these were just the "uppers." To enable me to fall asleep (since the loss of consciousness meant death, to me), I tried Lexomil (in France), Halcion, Clonodine, Lithium, Klonopin, and Atavan—and there were so many more. I've appreciated the candidness of those psychiatrists who have stressed the experimental nature of drug therapy, although, at times, when I'm floundering and nothing seems to work, I feel like we're "caught in a laboratory without a science."[25]

According to a recent article in the *New York Times*, the latest theory about diseases of the brain holds that "the deep sadness in severe depression, the hand wringing in obsessive compulsive disorder, the ringing in the ears of tinnitus, the unrelenting discomfort of chronic pain and the shaking and immobility seen in Parkinson's disease all stem from the same basic brain defect: a decoupling of two brain regions that normally fire their cells in synchrony."[26] The solution to all these ills, apparently, is the surgical implantation of electrodes into the thalamus (which has already been tried—with success). So why go through years of agonizing therapy when such a quick fix is available? Would it be, somehow, "cheating," like getting liposuction instead of dieting and taking aerobics classes to achieve the same physique (or like taking steroids to build muscle strength for competitive sports)? But if the same psychological effects can be achieved one way or the other, is there really anything other than squeamishness and financial considerations to be taken into account?

In writing the fourth edition of their *Diagnostic and Statistical Manual* (*DSM IV*), the American Psychiatric Association expressly aimed to keep the manual free of "theory" (meaning, primarily, psychoanalytic theory). There is, nonetheless, an implicit theory informing the description of mental disorders in the manual and that is biological reductionism—a theory motivated by the concomitant pressures for scientific respectability, medical diagnosis, and pharmaceutical intervention reimbursable by HMOs and other insurance companies. But these disorders are, at least to some extent, socially constructed, for political reasons. Even if it could claim to have achieved the status of a scientific discipline, the profession of psychiatry is not, in categorizing disorders, carving nature at its joints.

I agree with Ian Hacking (1995) that in the case of categorizations of creatures who are able (and indeed likely) to change according to our perceptions and expections of them (and theirs of themselves), there is the ever present possibility of a looping mechanism from the categorization to the thing being categorized. Some of this seems to go on. There is *some* truth to the charge that feminist psychotherapy—or, rather, as I would put it, only the misguided, distorted version of it—"turns women into victims," subtly conveying to highly suggestible patients that their chances of recovery depend on their conformity to *DSM IV* criteria of some diagnosable disorder or other. There may well exist a phenomenon of clinically directed psychic-morphing—a kind of "adaptive symptom formation."[27] It needn't be conscious, let alone willful, although if William James is right and we really can will ourselves to believe things we're not initially cognitively disposed to believe (but think it would be in our best interest to believe), it would be prudent for a patient—or would-be patient—to get her symptoms to conform to those of a disease meeting the criteria set for "serious" treatment, including insurance coverage.

But I disagree with those, such as Lamb, who believe that a clinical diagnosis of PTSD is "[o]ne of the worst thieves of victim agency/victim resiliency," one that comes perilously close to labeling the victimized woman as "damaged—or 'damaged goods' as the older, viler saying used to go" (1999, 111–112). In my experience, a diagnosis of PTSD (and subsequent treatment) can be empowering to a victim whose efforts to recover have been hindered by her (and society's) belief that her injuries are "all in her head." It can be more enabling to learn to work around—or to overcome—the symptoms of PTSD than it is to pretend that they are simply not there. Unless one accepts an extreme form of Cartesian dualism, holding that anything in the realm of the neurological is mechanistically determined, and therefore inevitable, whereas anything in the realm of the mental is under our control, it is implausible to suppose that such a medical diagnosis condemns to helpless passivity those so diagnosed.

Given a symptom—say, my still greatly exaggerated startle response (just yesterday I jumped at the sound of what turned out to be a leaf blowing along the sidewalk behind me)—I can say:

1. it was caused by the assault (which rewired my brain);
2. it was caused by some genetic predisposition to anxiety (my unaltered hardwiring); or
3. it was freely chosen by me.

Which of these is true? There's evidence for each hypothesis:

1. I didn't use to jump at such slight stimuli.
2. Yet someone who was constitutionally more serene might not have had this response after being attacked or, at any rate, might not still have it ten years later. This is *my* distinctive (although not unique) way of responding to such an attack.
3. It's hard to argue that this response was (the first time it occurred, anyway) freely chosen by me. I didn't even know at the time (while still in France, two weeks after my assault) about PTSD; nonetheless, I jumped. But one could argue that I now choose it, or at least put up with it. If I took tranquilizers, I would certainly be less reactive to such stimuli. (I would also be so lethargic as to be unable to write this and would probably spend most of my time in bed.) I've made the choice to function as actively as I can, out in the world, knowing that my nervous system is set at a precariously high level of sensitivity. It doesn't take much for the input-monitoring needle to tilt into the red—danger—zone. This is just what it is, for me, now, to be alive.

So what's the best hypothesis for why I jump at the sound of a dry leaf skittering down a sidewalk? I suppose it depends on who wants to know. If it's the crime victims' compensation board or my insurance company, this symptom was definitely caused by the assault. It's a physical condition—and not a preexisting one—treatable by scientifically established (and rather expensive) medical means.

If my therapist is trying to figure out what causes this symptom, in order to make it more manageable for me, it may make most sense to look at my underlying psychological predispositions. After all, another patient might have very different sequelae from a similar assault: obsessive-compulsive disorder, alcoholism, perhaps, or some other form of substance abuse. Why do I respond in *this* way? How might *I* be gotten to respond in a healthier way?

81
—
Acts of
Memory

If I'm the one trying to explain, and, ultimately, to eliminate this symptom, it may be best for me to take responsibility for it and to give myself a good talking to. But, then again, it might not. It may be that the stance that gives me most control over the symptom is the one I think appropriate for my therapist or my insurance company. Rather than beating my head against a wall, trying to will myself into having a different reaction, I can choose to take a pill to moderate my response. Or I can analyze why, given my early environment, I'm inclined to *this* sort of response.

Were my brain wired differently, as a result of nature or nurture, I might be better off taking a different sort of pill, or no pill at all. But this is the nervous system I have to work with. And this symptom is a current feature of my nervous system, something I can work with, work around, work through—but not something I can ignore or will to go away. To the extent that it impedes me in the attempt to engage in significant activities, it's a kind of disability. Not to attempt to treat it would be as silly as my trying to navigate my way around the world without my contact lenses.

My bad eyesight is not a disability (in my line of work) because it's treatable (more or less—I can't seem to get better than 20/30 correction) and because myopia and astigmatism are not stigmatized conditions (perhaps because so many academics have them). My PTSD is treatable (more or less), but it's a stigmatized condition (although I'm no more—or less—crazy than most people in my profession). Why? Because it's assumed that it, being a mental condition, is, or ought to be, under my control. Well, it is, in that I can choose whether and how to treat it, in the same way my vision is under my control. I could, after all, choose not to correct my vision. (I couldn't drive. I couldn't even walk. But if I were fed and otherwise taken care of, I could survive.) Not to wear glasses (or contact lenses) would be viewed as crazy. Why? Because treatment is available to bring me (almost) up to the norm. Trying to tough it out without glasses—to will myself to function in spite of my near-blindness—would not be courageous. It would be crazy.

Not to treat my PTSD would strike me as just as crazy. But the difference here is that, in order to get treatment, I have to "admit" that I have a mental illness. No one has to "admit" to being nearsighted. Is this because I could, if I tried really, really hard, just get over the PTSD? Granted, the interplay between our messages to ourselves ("buck up!" "relax") and our neurochemistry is such that a private pep talk can change the chemical composition of the wash and swirl of our neurotransmitters. So can a pill. This raises the age-old problem of mind-body reductionism. I'm not about to solve it and fortunately I don't need to. I can take a pragmatic approach. Sometimes, it works to think of myself as a mechanical system. Sometimes, it works to think of myself as a perceiver and maker of meaning. Sometimes thinking of myself as an agent with free will helps and sometimes, especially when the scope of the will is exaggerated, it doesn't. (At times telling myself to "buck up" just leads to a debilitating kind of neurochemical backfiring.)

The limits of my will are a mystery to me, but I know I can at least introduce some perturbations in my brain. I can do it by smiling, talking with a friend, having a scotch, jogging, screaming, taking a pill, reading a book, undergoing therapy, staying awake, going to sleep. It's up to me! Well, it's up to me in the same way that it's up to me whether or not to put on my glasses in the morning. I can choose to see or not to see. I can, to some extent, choose to be well or to be sick.

Acting in such a way as to make one acted upon (by drugs) can enhance agency—it can enable one to get out of bed, go out of the house, engage with a world that is no longer overwhelming. Being passive—allowing oneself to be acted upon—may be necessary for truly effective agency.

We are our molecules; our deepest fears, joys, and desires are embodied in the chemical signals of our neurotransmitters. But we are also creators of meaning, making up—and made out of—our histories, our idiosyncracies, our crazy plot-lines, our unpredictable outcomes. How are we to make sense of the fact that we are both?

Like one who seeks to warn the city of an impending
flood, but speaks another language. . . . So do we come
forward and report that evil has been done us.
—Bertolt Brecht[1]

The Politics of Forgetting

CHAPTER FIVE

A few months before my assailant's trial, I went to Grenoble to look over legal documents and discuss the case with my lawyer. I also met with the *avocat général*, who had possession of the dossier for the case and, with some reluctance, agreed to show it to me. It included depositions, police records, medical reports, psychiatric evaluations, and photos of my bruised, swollen face and battered body, of my assailant's scratched face, which I'd remembered so well, and of his muddied clothes, which I'd never really noticed. There were also photographs of the disturbed underbrush by the roadside, my belt found in the woods, and footprints in the mud at the bottom of the ravine where I had been left for dead. After our discussion of how the case would most likely proceed, as I was about to leave his office, the *avocat général* stunned me with these parting words of advice: "When the trial is over, you must forget that this ever happened."

I protested that forgetting such a traumatic event is not an easy thing for a victim to do. He then looked at me sternly and said, "But, *Madame*, you must make an effort." As if this had been simply an isolated event, of concern only to me. Perhaps *he* could have forgotten, but given the stories of rape I'd grown up with and the ones I'd heard and read about again and again in adulthood, one might say I remembered the rape even before it happened, as a kind of postmemory, to adapt Marianne Hirsch's term, informing the way I lived in my body and moved about in the world.[2] There would be no forgetting it now.

When I wasn't being exhorted to forget the assault, I was often told *how* to remember it. My own lawyer, meeting with me toward the end of my hospitalization in Grenoble, attempted to turn it into an individual, impersonal, as well as apolitical trauma with this unsolicited advice: "Don't think of your assailant as a human being. Think of him as a wild animal, a beast, a lion." I thought of him as a Frenchman, like my lawyer, but I said nothing and he continued: "Every morning when you waken, think of the new day as a gift." (He stopped short of saying "and rejoice and be glad in it," but it was clear that I was supposed to focus, henceforth, on my good fortune.) "Remember," he said, "you're not supposed to be alive."

Such attempts to obliterate (or to appropriate) my memories of the assault, however well-intentioned, collided with my own efforts to come up with a narrative of the trauma. I argued in chapter 2 that understanding trauma, including that of rape, requires one to take survivors' first-person narratives seriously as an essential epistemological tool. In this chapter I discuss the challenges of constructing a first-person rape narrative out of traumatic memories, and I explore some of the moral and political hazards involved in the use—and in the neglect—of such narratives.

Girls in our society are raised with so many cautionary tales about rape that, even if we are not assaulted in childhood, we enter womanhood freighted with postmemories of sexual violence. The postmemory of rape not only haunts the present, however, as do the postmemories of children of Holocaust survivors, but also reaches into the future in the form of fear, a kind of prememory of what, at times, seems almost inevitable: one's own future experience of being raped. Postmemories (of other women's rapes) are transmuted into prememories (of one's own future rape) through early and ongoing socialization of girls and women, and both inflect the actual experiences and memories of rape survivors.

Postmemories of rape are not primarily inherited from one's parents, but, rather, absorbed from the culture. Sometimes, the memory of particular cultural representations of events, as in films or computer imagery, stands in for, and seems more vivid than, the events themselves, as when Hillary Rodham Clinton "said the stories [of ethnic Albanians fleeing Kosovo] echoed images of the Nazi era, as depicted by films like 'Schindler's List' or 'Sophie's Choice.'"[3] Such culturally encoded memories (of sexual violence in film, on TV, in video and computer games, etc.) could play a large role in what I am here labeling the "postmemory" of rape.

Talk of "prememory" of rape is sure to be controversial: the idea is as baffling as that of backwards causation—or anticipation of the past. Memory follows time's arrow into the past, whereas anticipation, in the form of fear or desire, points to the future. So how could one possibly remember the future? One way of trying to make sense of this paradox is to note that fear is a future-directed state and that it is primarily fear that is instilled by postmemory of rape. The backward-looking postmemory of rape thus, at every moment, turns into the forward-looking prememory of a feared future that someday *will have been*—a temporal correlate to the spatial paradox of the Möbius strip, in which what are apparently two surfaces fuse, at every point, into one.[4]

Although I had been primed, since childhood, for the experience of rape, when I was grabbed from behind and thrown to the ground I initially had no idea what was happening. As I've mentioned earlier, I first experienced the assault as a highly unrealistic nightmare from which I tried to wake up. Then I realized that it was a rape-in-progress and I attempted to enact a range of rape-avoidance scripts I'd read about. After the first murder attempt, I experienced the assault as "torture-resulting-in-murder" and, unconsciously recalling Holocaust testimonies, I heard my assailant speaking in what I later described as a "gruff, Gestapo-like voice." Since I was not familiar with a literature of generic attempted-murder-victim narratives, I framed my experience in terms of a genre with which I *was* familiar.[5]

As long as I could make enough sense of the event to find something to say, I felt I had a chance of surviving. There was even a moment of relieved recognition when my assailant began sexually assaulting me. "OK, I see, this makes (some) sense." It suddenly became oddly familiar. "I've been through this before," I thought, although I hadn't. "Just follow his orders. Give him what he wants and he'll leave me alone." (This strategy didn't work, however, nor did that of fighting back, which was my body's idea.) Even later, when I thought he was going to kill me to prevent me from talking about the rape, I managed to think of things to say, such as the story that I'd been hit by a car and the line that "my friends will come looking for me, and it will be worse for you if they find me dead." But when, after being beaten and choked into unconsciousness several times, I realized that what he wanted was my death, when I pleaded with him not to kill me and he kept repeating "*il le faut*"—"I have to," "It must be done"—there was no more script for me to follow. I had to fight like prey pursued by a stronger predator— outrun him or outwit him, using animal instincts, not reason. After his last strangulation attempt, I played possum and he walked away. (When I could no longer hear his receding footsteps, I climbed up the ravine, hid in the underbrush by the side of the road, and, when a tractor [finally] approached, I stood directly in front of it so that the driver would have to stop for me whether he wanted to give me a ride or not.) As much as I later disagreed with my lawyer's characterization of my assailant as "a wild beast," that is how my body had categorized and responded to my attacker when there was no hope for human communication.

Although I experienced and remembered my assault under a wide variety of descriptions, it was, perhaps because of the cultural context, easiest for me to categorize the assault as a gender-motivated bias crime. Not only did the assault resonate with my postmemory of rape, confirming that, yes, women are all vulnerable to sexual violence, but the immediate aftermath heightened my sense of helplessness as a woman. I was, after climbing out of the ravine, surrounded mainly by men—the farmer driving the tractor, his neighbors, the doctor, the police officer, the ambulance driver, and the rescue personnel. They were all kind and helpful. (I recall especially the gentleness—tenderness, almost—of the young man who held the oxygen mask to my face in the ambulance all the way to the hospital.) At the hospital, more men waited to assist me—doctors, the police, the gendarmes, a prosecutor, a judge, more doctors. I was impressed by the concern, the competence, the solicitousness, of (almost all) the men in charge. But they were men—and they were in charge.[6]

I felt like a pawn—a helpless, passive victim—caught up in a ghastly game in which some men ran around trying to

kill women and others went around trying to save them—
rescuing them in tractors and ambulances, pushing them on
gurneys, giving them oxygen and injections and pills and
examinations, taking depositions, doing detective work,
making composite portraits, showing mug shots, tracking
down assailants, and writing up news reports. I did see some
women: a young mother, at the farmhouse I was taken to,
who held me close and tried to comfort me, and, at the
hospital, several nurses and a psychiatrist. The nurses treated
me tenderly, like a daughter, referring to me as the "*jeune
fille*" who'd been attacked. One of them told my husband
she thought I was in my early twenties.[7] (I was thirty-five.) I
used to think of myself as younger than my chronological
age, but, suddenly, having been so close to death, I felt
elderly, at the end of my natural life-span. (In my mental
snapshot album, I see a series of photos of a vibrant young
girl, followed by a group of shots of a careworn old woman,
punctuated, in the middle, by a grotesque Cindy Sherman-
like photograph of my bruised, swollen face, encrusted with
blood and dirt and leaves, looking like that of a corpse.)

Although I experienced the murder attempt as a sexual
violation, I was initially reluctant to tell people (other than
medical and legal personnel) that I had been raped. Using
the word "rape" would have conventionalized what happened to me, denying the particularity of what I had experienced and invoking in others whatever rape scenario they
had already constructed. When Tom, who had called my
parents to tell them of the assault, was asked by my father if
I had been raped, he said "no," largely to protect them. But
he had also been taken aback by the question. What difference did *that* make, he thought, since it was not yet clear
that I would even survive? My father's question was understandable though—motivated by a need to know *why* I had
been attacked.

I later asked Tom not to tell family and friends that I
was raped. I still wonder why I wanted the sexual aspect of
the assault—so salient to me—kept secret. I was motivated,
in part, by shame, I suppose, and I wanted to avoid a too-

easy stereotyping of myself-as-victim. I did not want academic work (that I had already done) on pornography and violence against women to be dismissed as the ravings of an "hysterical rape victim." Also, I felt I had very little control over the meaning of the term "rape." People would think they knew what had happened if they labeled the assault that way—their postmemories or the available cultural tropes would fill in the description—but they wouldn't. I later identified myself publicly as a rape survivor, having decided that it was ethically and politically imperative (for me) to do so. But my initial wariness about the use of the term was understandable and, at times, reinforced by others' responses—especially by the sexist characterization of the rape by some in the criminal justice system. Before my assailant's trial, I heard my lawyer conferring with another lawyer on the question of victim's compensation from the state.[8] He said, without irony, that a certain amount was typically awarded for "*un viol gentil*" ("a gentle rape") and a somewhat larger amount (which they would request on my behalf) for "*un viol méchant*" ("a nasty rape").[9]

Not surprisingly, I felt I was taken more seriously as a victim of a near-fatal murder attempt. But that description of the assault provided others with no explanation of what happened, no motivation on the part of my assailant. Later, when people asked me *why* this man tried to kill me, I revealed that the attack began as a sexual assault, and most people were satisfied with this *as an explanation*. It made some kind of sense to them. But it made no sense to me. Although the most succinct and accurate description of what occurred now seems to me to be "attempted sexual murder,"[10] it still makes little sense to me, even though I am now more aware (than I was before the assault) of the genre (of crime, of pornography, of literature, of art) of sexual murder.

I had been aware of the genre of "snuff films" and violently misogynistic cartoons, such as the one that appeared in the May 1983 issue of *Penthouse* depicting a man penetrating a woman from behind and holding a pistol to the back of her head. The caption reads: "Oh, you don't have to worry about getting pregnant. I've taken all of the precautions."[11] And I had gathered the genre went back at least as far as the middle ages, since I'd learned, as a teenager, such gruesome folk songs (allegedly of medieval origin) as "Pretty Polly." ("I courted Pretty Polly the live-long night [repeat], then left her next morning before it was light" [left her in a shallow grave, that is].)[12] Somehow, it didn't bother me to sing that or other songs of sexual violence (typically sung in the voice of the perpetrator) until I was assaulted. A while afterwards, a friend who was playing folk music with me started to sing "Tom Dooley." ("Met her on the mountain, 'twas there I took her life, met her on the mountain, stabbed her with my knife.") I found I could not sing along. Later I had to drop out of an aerobics class I was taking (to help me regain my strength) when the young female instructor persisted in playing a song I remembered well from my adolescence, with the refrain:

> You better run for your life if you can, little girl,
> Hide your head in the sand, little girl,
> Catch you with another man, that's the end, uh-little
>   girl.

The verses included such lines as "I'd rather see you dead, little girl, than to see you with another man."[13] The cognitive and emotional dissonance of watching a gym full of college-age girls bounce up and down to those lyrics was too much for me to bear.

I know I've become more sensitive to this genre, most broadly described as "sexual murder as entertainment," but sometimes I think it has also become more ubiquitous, more mainstream. In a broadcast the day after the Columbine High School massacre, Howard Stern joked about sexual murder, saying, "There were some really good looking girls running out with their hands over their heads. Did those kids [the suspects] try to have sex with any of the good looking girls? They didn't even do that? At least if you're going to kill yourself and kill all the kids, why wouldn't you have some sex?"[14]

Enough people must find these kinds of comments funny enough to keep Howard Stern on the air. Certainly, many others are revolted by such "humor," but probably most people don't find their brains disordered by such jokes, as I do. After hearing about many women who were killed during sexual assaults, and after getting to know a number of women who survived sexual murder attempts, I can't hear such things without thinking of particular victims, such as the woman who called me several years ago just before she went into the hospital to have a piece of plastic put into her head so that her brain could be protected where part of her skull had been sliced off by her machete-wielding assailant. Just minutes after I'd gotten off the phone with her that morning, I came across a book review in the Sunday *New York Times*. The author of the book was quoted in an interview as saying that the Marquis de Sade "writes about the instinct that makes us watch live footage of a man kill his wife on television, and derive some pleasure from it."[15] (Instinct *in us?* Who does he mean by "us"? Those who enjoy "high culture," who are above chuckling over the likes of Howard Stern?)

Since sexual violence has been considered, in so many different contexts, to be trivial or titillating, it's no wonder that many feminist theorists and legal reformers in the 1970s and 1980s made such an effort to reconceptualize rape as *violence*, not *sex*.[16] The "is rape violence or is it sex?" debate among feminists has always seemed pointless to me, however, and I think that, finally, the rape as sex versus rape as violence dichotomy is increasingly viewed as untenable. Rape is sexual violence. By this I don't mean that it is necessarily arousing (even to the perpetrator) and I don't mean that it is experienced *as sex* by the victim, but it is violence committed (typically) on the basis of sex (or because of the sex of the victim). It is different from other forms of violence in that respect.

Even now, I'm not sure just what led to my publicly calling myself a "rape survivor." It was at least partly motivated by my recognition, during my participation in the Philadelphia rape survivors' support group, of my comparative privilege and credibility. I realized that I had all the advantages, from a public relations point of view, that a rape survivor could have: I'm a white, well-educated, married, middle-aged, financially secure professional, who was wearing baggy jeans and a sweatshirt when attacked in a safe place in broad daylight. I was badly beaten. My assailant was apprehended and had confessed to the crime. It seemed inexcusably selfish to worry about *my* credibility when I compared myself to, say, a young black woman or a heroin addict or a prostitute in my support group. We were all brutally raped. We all thought we were going to die. Their stories were just as credible as mine. But, through no merit of my own, I was in a far better position (than most of the women in the group) to tell my story. Perhaps my telling it—if I could only tell it in the right way—would make it easier, someday, for others to tell theirs.

But, as I mentioned in chapter 2, constructing rape narratives in the first person is fraught with hazards—hazards that are risks of all first-person narratives of group-based trauma. Those of us writing (and using in our scholarship) first-person narratives of group-based traumas have to be careful not to speak only for ourselves, while avoiding speaking, without adequate knowledge or authorization, for others. We also need to question common assumptions about identity and acknowledge our multiple, shifting, intersecting identities. At different times and for different purposes, I have identified myself as a crime (attempted murder) victim, a rape survivor, a hate crime survivor, a person with a disability (PTSD and some other, stress-triggered neurological malfunctions), among other categories. The groups with which I identify expand (from rape survivors to all trauma survivors), contract (victims of attempted sexual murder), expand in other ways (hate crime survivors), contract (rape survivors), and so on, seemingly endlessly. After a period of focusing on trauma in general, I am now focusing, more narrowly, as I did initially, on the sexual aspects of my assault. Yet, at times, I seem to have more in common with some male victims of racist, or of homophobic, violence than I have with some women who have been raped. So much for identity politics. But for me to remember—and to narrate—my assault, it has to be remembered under *some* description or other, and not under all possible ones at once.

I've also found that people from a wide range of different groups identify with me, on reading what I've written about my assault. I've heard not only from rape survivors, but also from men and women who survived other sorts of crimes or debilitating diseases or accidents, from parents whose children have died, and, just recently, from a convicted murderer serving life in prison who (in an eight-page single-spaced letter) argued that he, like me, suffered from post-traumatic stress disorder, which supposedly explains why he killed a man without ever having intended to. All of these people found themselves sufficiently *like me*, in their traumatization, to say that my narrative had somehow illuminated their experiences.

If we are socially constructed, as I believe we are, in large part through our group-based narratives,[17] the self is not a single, unified, coherent entity. Its structure is more chaotic, with harmonious and contradictory aspects, like the particles of an atom, attracting and repelling each other, hanging together in a whirling, ever-changing dance that any attempt at observation—or narration—alters.

A further hazard of narrating trauma, is that of perpetuating one's self-definition as victim and others' stereotypes of one's group as weak and helpless.[18] Another way of expressing this hazard, with reference to rape narratives, is that there is a risk of instilling needlessly stifling postmemories in those who hear or read such narratives. Several years ago, numerous self-described feminists lamented the proliferation of rape narratives on the grounds that discussions of violence against women led to exaggerated fear and passivity on the part of women. I reacted to these writings, first, with disbelief, then with anger. Just when rape survivors were finding their voices, telling their stories (at last), people (feminists!) were telling them to shut up. I'm now more aware of the risk they warned of. I don't want to inflict any unnecessary burdens on women, and I don't want to contribute to the constriction of women's erotic desires or fantasies.

Rape affects the victim's views about sex, about herself as a sexual being, about men in general, about some men in particular. And an encounter with sexual murder (even if merely attempted) can completely (if only temporarily) shatter any assumptions a victim may have had about the connection between sex and love. If even *some* men have sex with women as a prelude to killing them, what does this say about sex? about men? about murder? To say I was put off by sex for a while would be a huge understatement. And my attitude didn't strike me as irrational. I was surprised more women didn't have it by virtue of merely having heard about sexual murder. Imagine, I thought, that I'd learned that some tennis players, after a game, kill their opponents—that something *about the game* seems to precipitate murder in some (not always predictable) circumstances. Why *should* I ever be inclined to play tennis again? Not only would the pleasure of playing not be worth the risk, but it is not clear what pleasure would be left in the game.

The memory of rape can thus make pleasurable erotic anticipation impossible: the past reaches into the present and throttles desire before it can become directed toward the future. I mourned my loss of sexual desire for years before it gradually started to return, as my fear diminished enough to make some psychic space for it. By the time I started speaking out about my rape, I considered telling my story to be a moral imperative (for me, not for every victim); but I also realized there were moral risks in speaking out. For example, why would I want to subject other women to anything like this loss of desire by contributing to their postmemory of rape with a gory trauma narrative of my own? (One might classify the genre of rape memoirs as *anti*-erotica.)

I'm torn between the moral imperative to testify about rape "so it never happens again" (although I know full well it is, at every moment, happening again) and the desire *not* to participate in the instilling of potentially destructive pre-memories. I want to help change the prevailing cultural tropes about sexual violence so that girls don't have to grow up in unduly constricted imaginary and real worlds.

Emmanuel Levinas asks, after discussing the vertigo felt by those who experienced the Holocaust, "Should we insist on bringing into this vertigo a portion of humanity whose memory is not sick from its own memories?" (1996, 120). He answers this question in the affirmative, and I have to agree with him, especially since one must educate future generations about the Holocaust if one is to have a chance of preventing it from happening again. But I remain unsettled by Kaja Silverman's (1996, 189) observation that "If to remember is to provide the disembodied 'wound' with a psychic residence, then to remember other people's memories is to be wounded by their wounds."

Still, I believe there is an imperative to tell my narrative of rape. In not telling one's narrative, one risks acting out the trauma—and causing others to act it out via their post-memories. Telling the narrative is an essential component of working through the trauma. It's not a question, then, of whether to tell, but whom, how, when, where, and—we must be especially aware of this—why. Countering the *avocat général's* injunction to forget is the political necessity to bear witness to the injustice of sexual violence.

Rape has, all too often and for all too long, been considered a private, personal matter, and thus not worthy of public, political concern.[19] War, on the other hand, has been viewed as a paradigmatic public, political event. The historian Pamela Ballinger, for example, asserts that "war veterans and survivors of the Holocaust and the A-bomb" are distinguished from "survivors of incest and other abuse" by the fact that "[i]n the case of abuse victims, no overarching historical 'event' (particularly that of state-sponsored violence . . .) exists within which individual memories may participate or contest. Rather, the event of abuse took place

privately. Its recollection, however, is facilitated by a broad
social environment obsessed with memory and in which
groups may jockey for benefits through appeal to collective
histories."[20] The moral relevance of such spatiotemporal
considerations is never made clear, however. What Ballinger
considers "private," that is, sexual, abuse, as opposed to collective violence, can be viewed instead as gender-motivated
violence against women, which is perpetrated against
women collectively, albeit not all at once and in the same
place. The fact that rape occurs all the time, in places all
over the world, may render it less noticeable as a collective
trauma, but does not make it an exclusively "individual"
trauma.

The one exception to the commonly held view of rape
as a private, individual matter, has been rape in war. Kuwaiti
women being raped by Iraqi soldiers in Kuwait City in 1990
was considered by some (Kuwaitis, pro–Gulf War U.S. law-
makers and citizens) to be a politically very weighty event,
and one requiring an international military intervention. (It
was *one* factor that was cited, anyway.) That many more
women were raped, during that time period, in the United
States was not viewed as a politically significant event, but,
rather, as simply part of life. The fact that the U.S. rapes
occurred (had occurred and would continue to occur) with
such frequency and in "our" neighborhoods obscured their
political import, making them seem natural, inevitable, and,
morally, not so bad.

> When evil-doing comes like falling rain, nobody calls out "stop!"
> When crimes begin to pile up they become invisible. When sufferings become
> unendurable the cries are no longer heard. The cries, too, fall like rain in summer.
> —Bertolt Brecht[21]

And so we must come forward and report that evil has been
done us. Doing so does not turn us—or others—into victims. It may be that the most debilitating postmemories are
those instilled by silence.[22] It is only by remembering and

narrating the past—telling our stories and listening to others'—that we can participate in an ongoing, active construction of a narrative of liberation, not one that confines us to a limiting past, but one that forms a background from which a freely imagined—and desired—future can emerge.

there's going to be a story, someone's going to try and
tell a story . . . my life and its old jingles . . . and what
I'm doing, all-important, breathing in and out and saying,
with words like smoke, I can't go, I can't stay, let's see
what happens next.
—Samuel Beckett[1]

Retellings

According to Aristotle, the first and most important element of a tragedy is the plot—the story, the narrative—defined as "an imitation of an action that is complete in itself, as a whole . . . which has beginning, middle, and end."[2] But narratives, at least those that are not tragedies, need not be linear or complete: a plot line could be a circle, a spiral, a parabola, a zigzag, a dot that went for a walk. A little walk that changes everything.

As I use the term, a "narrative" does not need to have a beginning, middle, and end, unless that is taken to mean, simply, that it starts and ends, with something in between. As Barbara Hernnstein Smith writes, a narrative is an act "consisting of *someone telling someone else that something happened.*"[3] It is a social interaction—actual or imagined or anticipated or remembered—in which what gets told is shaped by the (perceived) interests of the listeners, by what the listeners want to know and also by what they cannot or will not hear.

One of the most difficult narratives to hear is the telling of a trauma. It takes its toll on the listeners and it is not always therapeutic for the narrator. In earlier chapters, I described giving my testimony in court as "empowering" and "healing." And, in a sense, it was. In comparison to most other rape survivors, I was lucky, in being able to bring the perpetrator to justice. But, it seems to me now, there are ways in which having to get—and keep—a trauma narrative straight, for the purpose of a trial, for example, can also impede the process of recovery, hampering the ability to go on.

In the courtroom, what takes priority is the need for credibility as a witness, in order for justice to be done. In the therapist's office, by contrast, it's the need to acknowledge the harm to oneself, in order to heal from it and to figure out how to carry on. I felt I had done a good job of testifying at my assailant's trial when my lawyer praised me for getting my story just right ("exactly as you'd told it to me," he said), on having dotted all my *i*'s and crossed all my *t*'s. In contrast, I knew I was somehow failing at the therapeutic endeavor when, a couple of years earlier, a new therapist to whom I'd just told the story of my assault had said, "What a horrible experience. But you sound like you're describing something that happened to someone else."

What I emphasized earlier in this book as the central task of the survivor—regaining a sense of control, coming up with a coherent trauma narrative and integrating it into one's life story—may be crucial to the task of bearing witness, of living to tell, but it may, if taken too far, hinder recovery, by tethering the survivor to one rigid version of the past. It may be at odds with telling to live, which I now see as a kind of letting go, playing with the past in order not to be held back as one springs away from it. After gaining enough control over the story to be able to tell it, perhaps one has to give it up, in order to retell it, without having to "get it right," without fear of betraying it, to be able to rewrite the past in different ways, leading up to an infinite variety of unforeseeable futures.

My earlier discussions of the primary effects of trauma emphasized the loss of control and the disintegration of the (formerly coherent) self. My current view of trauma is that it introduces a "surd"—a nonsensical entry—into the series of events in one's life, making it seem impossible to carry on with the series. This account of the nature of trauma draws on both senses of surd—the mathematical sense (from the Greek *alogos*) of an irrational number or quantity, not expressible by an ordinary fraction, but only by an infinite series, and the linguistic sense of a voiceless sound or a sound dampened or deadened by a mute.[4] Charlotte Pierce-Baker conveys the trauma she experienced when she heard a crash or a thud one evening, shortly before being raped by two assailants who had broken into her home: "At that moment I knew the meaning of the word '*non*sense'" (1998, 29).

I thought I had made a certain sense of things until the moment I was assaulted. At any rate I thought I knew how to carry on with my life—to project myself, through action, into an imagined future—the way one knows how to go on in a series such as 2, 4, 6, . . . Not that there was a unique pattern leading ineluctably into a predictable future. The series could have been continued in any number of different ways: 2, 4, 6, 8, . . . or 2, 4, 6, 10, . . . or . . . But the assumption was that I could find *some* way of carrying on the narrative of my life. Trauma shatters this assumption by introducing an event that fits no discernible pattern: 2, 4, 6, square root of -2 . . . , say, or 2, 4, 6, ! . . . Not only is it now impossible to carry on with the series, but whatever sense had been made of it in the past has been destroyed. The result is an uneasy paralysis. *I can't go, I can't stay.* All that is left is the present, but one that has no meaning, or has, at most, only the shifting sense of a floating indexical, the dot of a "now" that would go for a walk, if only it knew where to go.

Narrative, I now think, facilitates the ability to go on by opening up possibilities for the future through retelling the stories of the past. It does this not by reestablishing the illusions of coherence of the past, control over the present, and predictability of the future, but by making it possible to carry on without these illusions.

The Trial

I'd been fairly confident of the verdict since the morning of my assailant's trial when my lawyer introduced me to the judge who'd clasped my hands, gazed at me briefly but knowingly, and said, "Don't worry, everything will be fine." Tom and I had entered the great halls of justice in Grenoble with my lawyer functioning as tour guide, his pride at the grandeur of the place overcoming any discomfort he may have felt over the occasion for my visit. These are the halls where Julien Sorel was tried, he explained, in *The Red and the Black*. As if, at that moment, I cared about anything other than what it would be like to see my assailant again, for the first time in two and a half years.

"I should warn you," the judge said to me that morning,

"you may not recognize your assailant. He's lost a lot of weight." It was true. When he was brought into the courtroom—slight, handcuffed, hardly menacing—he was accompanied by the warden and six armed guards. There was some small satisfaction in this—they weren't taking any chances—as well as a considerable amount of irony: *now* I have all this protection, when it's unnecessary and, really, a bit much under the circumstances. I was clearly no longer in any danger. Who were they protecting, anyway?

Still, when it was time for me to stand up front and give my testimony, I was grateful for their presence, for the uniforms, the guns, the judge's robes, the jurors in their precisely placed seats—the signs of law and order, of decorum, of "civilization," that had vanished during my assault. The props were all in place for me to tell my story. But how to tell it?

I must have felt some apprehension when I looked up from my berry picking on that morning walk and saw a man standing in a driveway just ahead, because I got up, crossed the road, made eye contact with the man, and said, "*Bonjour.*" He said "*bonjour*" back, which reassured me that the situation was safe. I kept walking. If he hadn't replied, or if he had looked menacing, perhaps I would have turned on my heels and run back where I came from. Or I would at least have looked over my shoulder to watch what he did next. But I didn't turn around, didn't look back, and I didn't even hear footsteps as he ran after me and slammed into my back, grabbing me from behind, his arms locked around mine, so that I couldn't strike back and I couldn't get out of his grip. (I learned later that he had been trained in hand-to-hand combat in the military.) I struggled and shouted "let me go" as he dragged me off the road, down a small slope, and into the underbrush. He threw me onto my back and, in a single motion, hit me hard with his fist just below my left eye, knocked out a contact lens, and shattered my ability to make sense of the world.

Living to Tell

The first narrative of the assault was the ever-shifting one I told to myself while it was in progress—this is a nightmare, no, this is a rape, no, this is a murder. The next narrative was the one I invented, in the subjunctive mode, for my assailant during the attack. I wouldn't say a word about him, about the attack, I told him. I would say I was hit by a car. I said this in response to his saying "I have to kill you," to explain why he didn't have to. When I then heard a rustling from the road above and I screamed as loud as I could, he was enraged that I was not to be trusted. "*Menteuse*," he hissed, "liar." My tale returned to haunt me when, after I was picked up on the road and taken to a nearby farmhouse, I said I was attacked by a man, and I could hear someone muttering, "She must have been hit by a car." Someone else, who found my story more plausible, stressed that "the attacker couldn't be from around here." It turned out that my assailant lived across the street.

My narrative varied as it was told to the farmer and his family, then to a police officer, a doctor, and the ambulance personnel, and, later, at the hospital, to Tom, more doctors, a psychiatrist, some gendarmes, my parents, a friend, another friend, then another. My story was shaped by what the listener needed to know most urgently, and, after a few days when I could breathe more easily, it expanded and contracted to fill whatever time was available.

The deposition I gave from my hospital bed took eight hours. If I'd had a different sense of the urgency of the situation or the patience of the officer transcribing what I said, it could easily have been much shorter or much longer. My first session with a psychiatrist took two and a half hours. (Of course, most subsequent sessions took forty-five or fifty minutes. But then I didn't attempt to tell the "whole" story.)

The listener's interest in the story provided the prompts, the questions, the responses, which, in turn, shaped the story. Sometimes the listener's particular interest led to peculiar questions, such as the one asked of me in the course of my deposition: "During the times you passed out, for how long did you remain unconscious?"

Less odd was the question about what my assailant wore, but I couldn't answer it. I was pressed to come up with something, to take a guess. I said the first thing that came to mind and soon knew my guess was wrong. "Oh, well," the officer said, "that doesn't matter." He then told me what my assailant had in fact been wearing. (His muddy, blood-stained clothes had been found in his home shortly after the assault.) It was clear the defense was never going to have access to this memory lapse. The officer's nonchalance just added to my disorientation. I thought the purpose of this deposition was to get at the truth (not only about what happened, but about my memory of what happened) in order to enable justice to be done. I began to sense that things (including the "official story") were being rigged from the start, *in order to* get my assailant convicted. Some things were left out and others (such as the description of me as "*sportive*") were *added* to my narrative by the officer to make it more convincing. The point was not, exactly, to get at the truth, unless "truth" is defined purely instrumentally as that which will help accomplish a goal, in this case, the goal of getting the suspect convicted.

The fact that I couldn't recall my assailant's clothes was understandable, given that I was focused only on survival during the assault. I felt so close to death during every conscious moment (after the first period of unconsciousness) that I didn't have the luxury to think, "Now, remember his clothes, that will be important for the trial." I didn't think about a trial, I didn't think about finding and arresting a suspect, I paid (absolutely focused) attention only to those aspects of my assailant I thought I needed to keep track of in order to survive. So, as it turned out, I did memorize his facial features so accurately that the composite portrait I constructed was a very close likeness.

After I constructed the portrait (with the aid of two

gendarmes from Lyon, who, apparently, had no knowledge of any suspects), the police soon returned to show me a photograph of the suspect and I immediately recognized my assailant. Sometime later (possibly even a day later, certainly several hours), they returned again to ask me to pick out his photo (the same one) from a lineup. Surely they were supposed to present his photo to me in this way the first time. It was disconcerting to realize that the defense would never know about this procedural mistake.

At the trial, the facts were not contested. The physical evidence showed there had been a rape and an attempted murder, that the man I'd recognized as my assailant was the perpetrator, and that I was the victim. Even the defense lawyer made a show of congratulating me on my strength and my courage. But my assailant had invoked the insanity defense. I was the only one who knew how he'd behaved by the side of the road, in the ravine, what he'd said, how he'd moved, how he was aware of what he was doing. He knew it was wrong and that he had to cover his tracks. I had to testify to all that.

When the verdict was announced—"On the charges of rape and attempted murder, the jury finds the defendant guilty"—I felt an instantaneous physical response: my body was shaking, wracked with sobs, although I didn't feel sad or elated. I didn't really feel anything but a sudden unclenching. I didn't have to keep the story straight. It didn't matter any longer if I got it right. I could let go of the details I'd kept alive in my mind, the narrative I'd remembered, rehearsed, and, finally, delivered to the court. "And how many times did you lose consciousness?" I'd been asked. "Four— twice from blows to the head, twice from strangulation attempts." "And the sexual assault?" "I was raped orally— '*Suce-le*', he'd ordered, repeatedly—not vaginally." My memory had served me (and the criminal justice system) well. A rapist and would-be murderer had been convicted. Now I could finally let down my guard, get fuzzy about the particulars, leave at least some of the horror behind, consign it to wherever they'd taken and left my clothes, my shoes, my belt, the fingernail scrapings, the hairs, the swabs, the leaves, the twigs, the mud, the blood. Now I could, in a sense, forget what had happened to me. Now I could afford to think about it.

Of course I'd thought about it, talked about it, written about it (dreamt, screamed, and wept about it) during the two and half years I waited for my assailant's trial. And I would never forget it. But now I could get a reprieve from the heightened lucidity that had led me to memorize my assailant's face during the attack, when my life had depended on reading every gesture, hearing every noise, taking everything down, storing it all away.

Had I not survived, my body would have borne silent, but powerful, witness to what happened during the assault. It might have served just as well, under the circumstances, as a witness for the prosecution. Someone could have told a story about it, made the flesh into words. (As it was, the photos of my battered face and body were an important part of the case, for the jury.) But *I* wanted to tell the story. I wanted the court to get it right, especially the part about my assailant's mental state at the time.

Still, there was something deadening about the requirement for truth. The snapshots preserved the image of my physical wounds, with no effort on my part, but only I could retain the memory of how I experienced the assault. Our conventions of justice require that a witness be viewed as presenting something as close to a snapshot as possible—a story unmediated and unchanging—from the perspective of a detached, objective observer. Although some accounts of traumatic memories associate the involuntariness of such memories with their (alleged) veridicality, in my case, it took some conscious effort to *will* the *true* story to stay straight in order to reproduce it at the trial.[5]

How might the need to keep a story straight in order to testify at a trial be connected to the compulsive repetition of a trauma narrative? It may be that the retroactive attempt to master the trauma through involuntary repetition is carried

—

out, intrapsychically, until a listener emerges who is stable and reliable enough to bear witness to it. Perhaps there is a psychological imperative, analogous to the legal imperative, to keep telling one's story until it is heard. After the story has been heard and acknowledged, one can let it go, or unfreeze it. One can unclench. What then happens to the story? Do we inevitably wound others with the transmission of our stories? There is some evidence that trauma, to the contrary, causes more harm to others (for example, subsequent generations) when transmitted through "untold stories" than when it is narrated (Bar-On 1995; Fresco 1984). Perhaps trauma gets defused in the telling, not only for survivors, but also for the listeners, in their retellings of stories that never make sense and so must be endlessly told.

Telling to Live

Just as there were different accounts of my assault, there are different stories of its aftermath. I thought when I began this book that it would incorporate a record of my recovery, charting my progress through the various stages—shock/dissociation; anger; integration—and analyzing the philosophical issues raised by each step of the process. And when I originally wrote about the therapeutic aspects of narrative, I was more optimistic in accepting the hopefulness and also the underlying view of the self in the psychological literature. My own trauma and recovery narrative was, initially, remarkably—uncannily—similar to what seemed to be becoming the standard rape narrative. But it isn't ending up that way.

The first few rape memoirs I read followed the expected plot—a kind of reverse-conversion narrative: "I once was found, but now am lost." A perfectly good, intact, life was destroyed, then painstakingly pieced back together.[6] This is how I first described my assault and recovery in "Surviving Sexual Violence," a piece largely conceived in the fall of 1990. My view was confirmed when I later read Judith Herman's *Trauma and Recovery* and I "recognized" that I had (already!) gone through the very stages of recovery she described. Although Herman rightly warned that "these stages of recovery are a convenient fiction, not to be taken too literally," it was comforting to think I was on a predictable path and nearing, if not actually at, the end. And it was a relief to learn that my reactions were not unusual. Since I had been getting the message (not only after my assault, but my entire life) that I was just "too sensitive," it was a relief to read that, according to Herman, "[t]he most powerful determinant of psychological harm is the character of the traumatic event itself. Individual personality characteristics count for little in the face of overwhelming events. There is a simple, direct relationship between the severity of the trauma and its psychological impact."[7] I wasn't crazy. I was *traumatized*. My responses were normal, to be expected, after such a terrifying event.

But then, after things got better, they got worse. I wasn't surprised that my recovery wasn't linear—no one led me to expect that—but by the fact that whatever trajectory my life was on didn't seem to *be* one of recovery.[8] There was (and is) no discernible pattern. I'd like to be able to tell a story of trauma and recovery in the more "conventional" sense. My unfolding narrative, however, has not only not been linear, or orderly in some other way, it is also constantly being revised, and is permanently revisable. There are several reasons for this: some emotional aspects of trauma cannot be experienced, and thus narrated, until the survivor has already made a certain amount of progress toward recovery (whatever that might be). I recall one therapist's comment: it's precisely because you're doing so well (making so much progress) that you're feeling so much worse. In addition, earlier events can come to have new meaning (or become meaningful for the first time) in light of insights gleaned from later events. Building the cognitive structure to hold a life's narrative takes time, and earlier bits need to be revisited. The past continually changes as new parts of the pattern of one's life emerge.

The course of my recovery has had more to do with what was going on around me at the time than with the amount of time elapsed. A year after the assault, I felt I had made enormous progress—until the death of my father-in-law and the reemergence of my traumatized self at his funeral. I remember: the open casket, my shock at seeing a dead person—no, at seeing people carry on conversations in the same room as a dead person, the heat, my faintness, my feebly singing the song he'd requested: "You'll Never Walk Alone." And then the procession to the cemetery, the reassurances that we wouldn't stay to see the burial, the lengthening shadows as the late afternoon graveside service ended and the condolences went on and on, my panic at seeing the casket lowered into the ground, my inability to say, to my husband, to my mother-in-law, "I have to get out of here, I can't breathe, I feel like I'm going into the earth with him." My shame at such self-centered reactions. The terror, the silence, the utter aloneness of death.

The graph of my recovery continued to oscillate over the next few years, registering the seismic tremors (of varying degrees) of more deaths, the trial, professional stresses, several moves. Then, four years after the assault, my spirits soared with the birth of my son. His arrival brought regeneration, joy, and the imperative to rebuild my trust in the world, to believe, in spite of everything, that the world is a good enough place for him to grow up in. I remember my astonishment at touching the crown of his head as I was giving birth: My God, I thought, as if for the first time, I'm having a *baby!* I knew I'd been pregnant—how could I not have known, after nine months of nausea and near-constant exhaustion? But I was truly surprised to discover that all this was culminating in a baby, a new life, my child. A while later I asked my therapist, over the phone, "How could I *not* have realized, even moments before, that I was going to give birth?" Her words, soothing and knowing, as always, made sense immediately: "You couldn't afford to believe it." Now, I was back among the living, with an obligation to carry on, with a commitment to hope. For a year and a half, I felt blessed.

But how can we ever afford to believe in our good fortune, in a world in which, as the old country-western song goes, "Just when things are going fine / Someone jumps you from behind"? Two days before Christmas 1995, I ran into a friend who had recently had surgery and chemotherapy for breast cancer. It was in remission and she was back at work, her stylishly short hair looking more perky than pathological. I expressed delight at her recovery and she just smiled and said, "Aren't we lucky?" I said, "Yes, we are," not merely to be polite, but meaning it, marveling at her good health and spirits and thinking of my one-year-old boy's delight in the snow and the big lighted tree and toy train in town, the thrill of new beginnings, my excitement at the thought of our first Christmas in our own home in Vermont. The next night, on the other side of the country, my brother killed himself by diving off the sixth floor of a hospital parking garage. The universe didn't catch him.

I'll never know how he lost whatever kept him tied to life. Distressed over a recent move, he became trapped in an intolerable present, fearing his future and unable to tell the story any other way. My father said he died of regret.

I can only speculate about his motivations. His story is not mine to tell. But the forcefulness of his final act reminded me of the words he chose to appear under his photo in his high school yearbook:

I am the master of my fate;
I am the captain of my soul.[9]

The only way he could be master of his fate was to make sure no one—and nothing—else would be.

My brother's ashes were mailed, in a box, from the hospital where he died to my parents' house. My mother told me that, at the committal ceremony, when the minister gently handed her the box, tiny as a newborn, she held it on her lap and wept. I know how my whole body winces when my child scrapes his knee. I imagine my mother sitting there, dissolving into dust and bone, disappearing with her beautiful boy into the mineral world of atoms and galaxies, of things too small or too large to be conceived, out into the realm of rocks and stones and stars.

My parents planted a tree in his memory. They tell me when it blooms each spring, around Mother's Day.

My brother's death introduced another surd into the series of events making up my life. When he slammed the book shut on his own narrative, I lost my own ability to speak. There's a risk in truly recognizing another's (possibly greater) pain. It can make one feel less entitled to one's own.

This wasn't the first time I had lost my voice. After my assault, I had frequently had trouble speaking. I lost my voice, literally, when I lost my ability to continue my life's narrative. I was never entirely mute, but I often had bouts of what a friend labeled "fractured speech," in which I stuttered and stammered, unable to string together a simple sentence without the words scattering like a broken necklace. During the assault itself, my heightened lucidity seemed to be accompanied by an unusual linguistic fluency—in French, no less. But being able to speak quickly and (so it seemed to me) precisely in a foreign language when I felt I had to in order to survive was followed by episodes, spread over several years, when I couldn't, for the life of me, speak intelligibly, even in my mother tongue.

For about a year after the assault, I rarely, if ever, spoke in smoothly flowing sentences. I could sing, though, after about six months, and, like aphasics who cannot say a word, but can still sing verse after verse, I never stumbled over the lyrics. I recall spending the hour driving home from my weekly rape survivors' support group meetings in Philadelphia singing every spiritual I'd ever heard. It was a comfort and a release. Mainly, it was something I could do, loudly, openly (by myself in a closed car), and easily, accompanied by unstoppable tears.

Even after I regained my ability to speak, more or less reliably, in English, I was unable to speak, without debilitating difficulty, in French. Before my ill-fated trip in the summer of 1990, I'd never have passed for a native speaker, but I'd visited France many times and spent several summers there. I came of age there, intellectually, immersing myself in research on French feminism in the late 1970s, which led to my interviewing Simone de Beauvoir (in Rome) one summer. It was also a place of sexual pleasure and expansiveness. I was freer in French, whether living on my own for the first time in Paris, singing French folk songs, sailing on Lake Annecy, hiking in the Alps, or stopping to buy cheese in a little village called *"Brison"* (and taking out my driver's license to help explain the reason for my pilgrimage). Now, over ten years after the assault, I still almost never speak French, even in Francophone company, in which I often find myself, given Tom's interests. My speech deficit is still much more pronounced in French than in English, which I suppose shouldn't be surprising, given that it's not unusual even for complete bilinguals, with neurological disorders such as aphasia, to lose the ability to speak (or comprehend) only one language.

My brother's death also made me rethink the importance of regaining control in recovering from trauma. Maybe the point is to learn how to relinquish control, to learn by going where we need to go, to replace the clenched, repetitive acting out with the generativity of working through. The former, although uncontrollable, is, paradoxically, obsessed with control, with the soothing, numbing safety of the familiar. The latter is inventive, open to surprise, alive to improvisation. The former can instill the dangerous, even deadly, illusion of invincibility. The other can provide the foundation of trust on which new life can be built, the steady bass continuo that liberates the other parts to improvise without fear.

What do I now make of the comment made by the facilitator of my rape survivors' support group: "You'll never be the same . . . , but you can be better"? I guess I still have to agree with it. Not "better" in the sense of having a life that's more coherent, in control, predictable. But "better" in the sense that comes from acknowledging that life is a story in the telling, in the retelling, and that one can have some control over *that*.

Recovery no longer seems to consist of picking up the pieces of a shattered self (or fractured narrative). It's facing the fact that there never was a coherent self (or story) there to begin with. No wonder I can't seem to manage to put myself together again. I'd have to put myself, as the old gag goes, "together again for the first time."

Philosophers speak of the importance of a rational life plan, of the human need to shape pointless absurdity into soul-satisfying meaning, progressively making sense of it all, right up to the end. I've never been able to reconcile this with the physicist's view of entropy as time's arrow. Anyone who has shared a home with a big project or a small child knows the Sisyphean nature of life, the endless, repetitive, futile attempt to impose order on chaos. "Why bother?" one might say, with joyful abandon or crushing despair.

Maybe recovery is reestablishing the illusory sense of the permanence of hope, learning how to be, once again, "crazy-human with hope."[10] As irrational as it is, I want to believe that, just as there is such a thing as irreparable damage, there might be such a thing as irreversible repair. Hope, like despair, can *feel* permanent. But more likely, the entropy of emotional life—governed by some inexorable law of psycho-dynamics—makes this impossible. Of course, the belief that things can, once and for all, be made right, makes no more sense than the belief (which takes hold of me, on average, once every few months) that everything is totally, irreparably, ruined. But does it make any *less* sense? For me, anyway, the illusion that hope will perch permanently in my heart is psychologically untenable—I just can't hold that happy thought for more than a day or two. But objectively—whatever that means—it's just as plausible, just as rational, as my more obdurate belief in psychic entropic doom.

Perhaps the goal of recovery is, simply, to go on. But—go on with what? With the series of my days, the pattern of my life? What pattern? The pattern to which it would have con-formed without the assault? Who knows what that would have been? The pattern before the assault? Who knows what that was? Some days there seems to be no pattern—just the odd refrain, a reprise, a recurring motif. *My life and its old jingles.* No meaning but the melody, the major or minor mode, the tune that carries me through until the lyrics come back.

There's one more retelling I have to do. I have to tell the story of my assault to my son. It won't be the hardest thing I have to tell him, but it won't be easy. The story I tell him must be a different telling, inflected by his needs and framed by his questions. It must be told in a way that doesn't toughen his skin and turn his tender heart to stone.

I understand a parent's pull toward silence. I'd like to spare him needless, and even needful, suffering. It was only as an adult that I learned that when my mother was fifteen her father was killed by a hit-and-run truck driver, and her mother said to her, "From now on, you are my rock." She was schooled, no doubt benevolently, in the ontology of silence, as if, without the words to say it, there wouldn't be so much pain.

I can't tell my son the story of my assault in the way I'd like, pretending it didn't really happen, or that it had a redemptive, happy ending. But my telling doesn't have to break him. It's not a tragedy. The story doesn't have an ending. The truth is, I'm not lucky or unlucky. I'm just alive. *Breathing in and out.*

"Tragedy," Wittgenstein wrote, "is when the tree, instead of bending, breaks."[11] What I wish most for my son is not the superhuman ability to avoid life-threatening disasters, but, rather, resilience, the capacity to carry on, alive in the present, unbound by dread or regret. Not the hard, flinty brittleness of rock, but the supple tenacity of the wind-rocked bough that bends, the bursting desire of a new-mown field that can't wait to grow back, the will to say, whatever comes, *Let's see what happens next.*

In memory of
Susanne and Half Zantop
and
Trhas Berhe and Selamawit Tsehaye

Be ahead of all parting, as though it already were behind
you, like the winter that has just gone by. For among
these winters there is one so endlessly winter that only
by wintering through it will your heart survive.
—Rainer Maria Rilke[1]

Afterword

On January 27, 2001, about six months after I had submitted this manuscript, two of my dear friends and colleagues, Susanne and Half Zantop, were stabbed to death in their home a few miles away from Dartmouth College. They were deeply loved members of this community—a wonderfully close-knit community of friends, scholars, social activists, and neighbors they had done so much, in over twenty-five years here, to create and sustain. Susanne had been my official and unofficial mentor at Dartmouth, standing by me for the past decade. She set the standard with her own stellar example and never wavered in her demanding expectations of me; when, in the wake of my assault, I felt like giving up on my academic career, she simply wouldn't hear of it.

A group of us had been planning to celebrate a birthday

with Susanne and Half at a brunch and sledding party one Sunday morning. Instead, those of us who hadn't heard about their deaths the night before read about them in the local newspaper. We gathered, stunned, in someone's home, as we did for days to come, holding on to each other and trying to make sense of what had happened. Was it a robbery? A case of a disgruntled student who'd gone berserk? Would anything ever make sense again?

I went to the New Hampshire Attorney General's press conference that afternoon with two friends. In the crowd of reporters and local residents, the questions buzzed: How could this have happened here? To them? To *us*? After the press conference, my friends stayed to speak to the reporters, not about the grisly deaths, but about the extraordinary lives of these two remarkable people. I couldn't speak, not without enormous difficulty, and so I stood off by myself. When I overheard some journalists speculating about when the last murders had occurred in Hanover—about ten years ago? 1990? I had just enough words in me to say, "It was in June of '91."

On the evening of June 16, 1991, there were, according to Joseph Harris, then chair of the Physics Department at Dartmouth, five black women Ph.D. candidates in physics in North America. The next morning there were three. Two of them, Trhas Berhe and Selamawit Tsehaye, had been ax-murdered in the night on a quiet Hanover street a block away from where I was living at the time. My husband and I had just moved back up that evening from Princeton, where I'd spent the academic year on a disability leave. That morning, I walked to a café by myself (just a few blocks from where we lived, but still a challenge) and saw the headline in the local paper. My already keen sense that no place in the world was safe was made only more vivid by this news. But as I walked back out into the bright summer light, it seemed that somehow those murders hadn't shaken the sense of security of most people in the community. Students returning for summer term played frisbee and sunned themselves on the green. Dogs chased balls, families shopped along Main Street, kids ate icecream cones. Alumni back for reunions paused to look at the ever-enticing real estate photos in sidewalk displays. Sure, there was some gossip (was it a crime of passion? wasn't the murderer the former boyfriend of one the victims?) but no one seemed particularly distraught. Life went on: I just couldn't remember why.

Even though I hadn't known the two women (they'd arrived while I was away, and I don't often get to know graduate students in the natural sciences here), I was devastated by their murders—and by the apparent (lack of) reaction in Hanover and elsewhere. (I think the *Boston Globe* had a paragraph or so about them, in one day's edition, but the murders weren't reported beyond that in the national press, as far as I know.) The day the murders were reported in the local papers, the Dartmouth flag (almost *always* at half-mast, it seems, to mourn the death of some former trustee or emeritus faculty member or wealthy alumnus) remained at full mast (until a day or so later). A week after the murders, I asked various administrators for funds to bring a women's self-defense and rape-prevention instructor to Dartmouth and the response was, "Why? Nothing ever happens here." These were just two of many signs that the murders were not going to be viewed as something that had happened "here," to "us."

The victims, as well as the perpetrator, were black—and Ethiopian—facts that seem to have made it easier for people to reassure themselves that this would never happen again, and, in some sense, never really *did* happen in our community. I was (perhaps naively) surprised at the lack of media attention to their murders. But now, given the almost daily international attention that's been paid to Susanne's and Half's murders, I'm outraged. Susanne and Half would have been among the first to point out—and to condemn—this disparity.

Before my own assault, I was able to distance myself from the brutal murders occurring daily around the world, and, sometimes, around the block. But at the memorial service for Trhas and Selamawit, presided over by the woman who had married Tom and me, in the same chapel on campus, I cried and cried. Of course it was in large part a self-regarding reaction, motivated as much by the memories their murders triggered in me as by my horror at what had happened to them. But I found it hard to separate these things. I felt I knew what they had known as they were about to die, and I realized their funeral could have been mine, that my survival could have been theirs, and that nothing explained or justified our different fates. I also wept through Susanne and Half's memorial service, officiated over by the same pastor, in the same place, and again I felt sheepish, guilty almost, at feeling so much grief over my friends' deaths. Was I really just mourning my own loss? my pain at having so nearly suffered the same fate? I couldn't help but think of their final moments together, in the last throes of life, when meaning flowed away like blood, and all that remained was the will to live, the pull toward death, the urge to wake, to sleep, to stay, to go, to know and not to know—their only ease their sharpest pain—they would not die alone.

I still can't bring myself to tell my son that Susanne and Half were murdered. I just said that they died. I have no story to tell about how such violence won't happen to us. It could. There's no way to prepare for it, to "be ahead of all parting." And there's no getting over it. All we can do is hold on fiercely to one another, "As the lost human voices speak through us and blend / Our complex love, our mourning without end."[2]

Overnight, it seems, spring has returned to Vermont. The fields are green, trees are in blossom, the pond is teeming, and the bluebirds are back. Life—profligate, irrepressible—flaunts itself everywhere. An overflowing of life, even for the least significant creatures—so much so that it all seems inevitable. Perhaps because it is impossible for us to imagine our own deaths, our existence can feel necessary, bound to continue. But maybe my lawyer was right: I should remember that I'm not supposed to be alive. What if I take that as my starting point? None of us is *supposed* to be alive. We're all here by chance and only for a little while. The wonder is that we've managed, once again, to winter through and that our hearts, in spite of everything, survive.

Thetford, Vermont
April 2001

Acknowledgments

It took me ten years to write this book—long enough, I fear, for my debts of gratitude to exceed my ability to remember them all. I hope I will be forgiven by those I have forgotten to acknowledge.

Much of the material in this book was originally presented in talks before philosophical as well as interdisciplinary audiences on the following occasions: The North American Society for Social Philosophy Annual Conference (Davidson College, August 1992); Annual Conference of the Indiana Coalition against Sexual Assault (Indianapolis, September 1993); Conference on Feminist Ethics and Social Policy (University of Pittsburgh, November 1993); Indiana University (September 1994); Conference on Women, Sexuality, and Violence (University of Pennsylvania, March 1995); American

Comparative Literature Association Conference (Puerto Va-llarta, Mexico, April 1997); Cornell University Society for the Humanities (March 1998); Conference on Memory, Post-memory, and Gender at the Minary Conference Center (Dartmouth College, June 1999); Society for Women in Phi-losophy—Pacific Division (Cabrillo College, Calif., October 1999); and the Larkin Lectures in Ethics (Mount St. Mary's College, Calif., March 2000). I benefited greatly from audience responses at these events.

I am grateful for the generous administrative support and funding I have received from Dartmouth College, in-cluding a disability leave, faculty research funds, a junior faculty fellowship, and a fellowship in the spring 1996 Dartmouth Humanities Institute on "Cultural Memory and the Present." The Women's Studies program at Dartmouth, coordinated by the incomparable Anne Brooks, provided me with an intellectual home as well as endless moral support while writing this book. My mentors in the Dartmouth Women's Faculty Mentoring Network, Brenda Silver and Susanne Zantop, and my unofficial mentor, Mary Kelley, showed me that I could write this book *and* get tenure—two goals that I, at times, thought were incompatible.

Much of this book was completed in the ideal work environment of the School of Social Science at the Institute for Advanced Study in Princeton, N. J., where I spent 1997–98 as an NEH-funded member and most of 1998–99 as a visitor. While at the institute, I received valuable feedback from many colleagues, including those in two reading groups: one on Trauma and Memory, which met in the spring of 1998, and another on Feminist Theory, which met in the spring of 1999.

For comments on earlier drafts of various chapters I am indebted to Carol Bardenstein, Lynda Boose, Claudia Card, Mary Childers, Jonathan Crewe, Susan Dwyer, Gerd Gem-unden, Atina Grossmann, Jodi Halpern, Sally Haslanger, Vir-ginia Held, Claudia Henrion, Susannah Heschel, Marianne Hirsch, Nancy Hirschmann, Amy Hollywood, Alexis Jetter, Karen Jones, Irene Kacandes, Debra Keates, Eva Feder Kittay,

Dominick LaCapra, Catriona Mackenzie, Karen McPherson, Diana Tietjens Meyers, Linda Mulley, Annelise Orleck, Eric Santner, Gordon Schochet, Joan W. Scott, Jonathan Shay, Charles Shepardson, Leo Spitzer, Natalie Stoljar, Diana Taylor, Wanda Teays, and Melissa Zeiger. Joan Bolker not only commented on earlier drafts, but also, from the moment I called her from the Grenoble hospital to the day I sent this book to press, reminded me that "the art of losing's not too hard to master / though it may look like (*Write* it!) like disaster."[1]

Many more people than I can name, in addition to those above, provided friendship and sustenance of various kinds. My thanks to them and to: Susan Ackerman, Amy Allen, Melissa Bailey, Marcia Baron, Omer Bartov, Helen Benedict, Leigh Bienen, Dr. John Blake, Bronwyn Brady, Dr. Hal Cash, Lorraine Code, Peggy Darrow, Judith DeCew, Heather Earle, Robert Elias, Bathsheba and James O. Freedman, Ann Gaulin, Ian Gold, Mary Jean Green, Dr. Gary Karpf, Charles and Marilyse Hamm, Ozzie Harris, Lynn Higgins, Perry Hodges, Deborah King, The Reverend Gwendolyn S. King, Jeffrey, Leo and Sesha Kittay, Carol Koffel-Yu, Drew Leder, Bernard Levinson, Wai-Yee Li, Shira Li-Bartov, Daniel Lieberfeld, Marie-Victoire Louis, Tom Luxon, Lynn Mather, Mary Kate McGowan, Janice McLane, Michelle Meyers, Monique Middleton, Diane Miliotes, Valerie Miller (and the Thetford Chamber Singers), Richard Moran, Bruce and Donna Nelson, Leslye Obiora, Evann and Raphael Orleck-Jetter, Agnes Lugo-Ortiz, Cathy Popkin, Ulrike Rainer, Linda Ramzy Ranson, Merelyn Reeve, Judith Sanders, Ivy Schweitzer, Suzanne Serat, Pi Smith, Silvia Spitta, Janis Strout, Lee Talley, Cynthia Taylor, Lynne Tirrell, Catherine Tudish, Lenore Walker, Cathy Winkler, James and Susan Wright, Half Zantop, and Yetta Ziolkowski.

I would like to thank Fred Appel, Maria denBoer, Ellen Foos, Mary Murrell, and Ann Wald at Princeton University Press for their editorial expertise; Tonya Blackwell, Margo Conti, Heidi Gamer, and Mattie Richardson for their research assistance; the students in my courses on violence against women for their insights and their commitment to social justice; William Fontaine for bibliographic help; Deborah Koehler and Sandra Curtis for administrative support; Susan Bibeau for computer advice; and Shifra Levine and the day care programs at Crossroads and U-Now (in Princeton) and Maple Leaf (in Thetford) for the loving child care that made my writing possible.

My parents, my sister, her family, and my husband's family supported me in every way they possibly could, for which I will always be grateful.

Several people read earlier versions of the entire book: Mieke Bal and Sara Ruddick, readers for Princeton University Press, who provided extremely insightful and extensive comments; Ann Bumpus, whose philosophical acumen and sense of fun helped me to think more rigorously and to laugh more often; Margot Livesey, who, in nearly twenty-five years of friendship, has deepened my love of writing and of life and taught me that neither needs to be a lonely enterprise; and Thomas Trezise, whose image once kept me alive and whose presence sustains me in more ways than I could have imagined. I dedicate this book to him and to our son, Gabriel.

Notes

Preface

    1. *The Random House Dictionary of the English Language*, 2nd ed., Stuart Berg Flexner, Editor in Chief; Lenore Crary Hawk, Managing Editor (New York: Random House, 1987), 36.

    2. Ursula K. LeGuin, *Dancing at the Edge of the World: Thoughts on Words, Women, Places* (New York: Grove, 1989), 7.

O N E   Surviving Sexual Violence

    1. Federal Bureau of Investigation, *Uniform Crime Reports for the United States*, 1989, 6.

    2. Robin Warshaw notes that "[g]overnment estimates find that anywhere from three to ten rapes are committed for every one rape reported. And while rapes by strangers are still underreported, rapes by acquaintances are virtually nonreported. Yet, based on intake observations made by staff at various rape counseling centers (where

victims come for treatment, but do not have to file police reports), 70–80 percent of all rape crimes are acquaintance rapes" (Warshaw 1988, 12).

3. National Coalition against Domestic Violence, fact sheet, in "Report on Proposed Legislation S.15: The Violence against Women Act," 9. On file with the Senate Judiciary Committee.

4. Another, much more perceptive, article is Lois Pineau's "Date Rape: A Feminist Analysis" (Pineau 1989). In addition, an excellent book on the causes of male violence was written by a scholar trained as a philosopher, Myriam Miedzian (Miedzian 1991). Philosophical discussions of the problem of evil, even recent ones such as that in Nozick (1989), don't mention the massive problem of sexual violence. Even Nell Noddings' book, *Women and Evil*, which is an "attempt to describe evil from the perspective of women's experience" (Noddings 1989), mentions rape only twice, briefly, and in neither instance from the victim's point of view.

5. See especially Patricia Williams' discussion of the Ujaama House incident in *The Alchemy of Race and Rights* (Williams 1991, 110–116), Mari Matsuda, "Public Response to Racist Speech: Considering the Victim's Story" (Matsuda 1989), and Charles Lawrence, "If He Hollers, Let Him Go: Regulating Racist Speech on Campus" (Lawrence 1990).

6. As the authors of *The Female Fear* note: "The requirement of proof of the victim's nonconsent is unique to the crime of forcible rape. A robbery victim, for example, is usually not considered as having 'consented' to the crime if he or she hands money over to an assailant [especially if there was use of force or threat of force]" (Gordon and Riger 1991, 59).

7. Robert Lowell, *Selected Poems* (New York: Farrar, Straus and Giroux, 1977), 82.

8. Quoted in the *New York Times*, September 13, 1991, A18. Although Judge Thomas made this statement during his confirmation hearings, Justice Thomas's actions while on the Supreme Court have belied his professed empathy with criminal defendants.

9. Barnes (1984, 2181–2182). 1 thank John Cooper for drawing my attention to this aspect of Aristotle's theory of the emotions.

10. For a clinical description of post-traumatic stress disorder (PTSD), see *DSM IV* (1994). Excellent discussions of the recovery process undergone by rape survivors can be found in Bard and Sangrey (1986), Benedict (1985), Herman (1992), and Janoff-Bulman (1992). 1 have also found it very therapeutic to read first-person

accounts by rape survivors such as Susan Estrich (Estrich 1987) and Nancy Ziegenmeyer (Ziegenmeyer 1992).

11. *Diagnostic and Statistical Manual of Mental Disorders*, 3rd rev. ed. (Washington, D.C.: American Psychiatric Association, 1987) 247. *DSM IV* no longer refers to the precipitating event in this way. Instead, it refers to "an extreme traumatic stressor" (*DSM IV* 1994, 424).

12. I was particularly interested in that section of the act which classified gender-motivated assaults as bias crimes. (This section of the act was, unfortunately, struck down by the U.S. Supreme Court in the spring of 2000.) From the victim's perspective this reconceptualization is important. What was most difficult for me to recover from was the knowledge that some man wanted to kill me simply because I am a woman. This aspect of the harm inflicted in hate crimes (or bias crimes) is similar to the harm caused by hate speech. One cannot make a sharp distinction between physical and psychological harm in the case of PTSD sufferers. Most of the symptoms are physiological. I find it odd that in philosophy of law, so many theorists are devoted to a kind of Cartesian dualism that most philosophers of mind rejected long ago. (See Brison 1998.)

13. *New York Times*, April 19, 1992, 36.

14. She characterized a certain theory of equality in this way during the discussion after a Gauss seminar she gave at Princeton University, April 9, 1992.

15. For an illuminating discussion of some of the ways in which we need to treat people differently in order to achieve genuine equality, see Minow (1990).

16. As recently as 1948, the U.S. Supreme Court upheld a state law prohibiting the licensing of any woman as a bartender (unless she was the wife or daughter of the bar owner where she was applying to work). *Goesaert v. Cleary*, 335 U.S. 464 (1948).

17. *New York Times*, June 19, 1992, 1, A13.

T W O   On the Personal as Philosophical

1. Bertrand Russell, *The Problems of Philosophy* (New York: Oxford University Press, 1969), 160.

2. Friedrich Nietzsche, *Beyond Good and Evil*, trans. Walter Kaufmann (New York: Vintage, 1966), 13. Orig. pub. 1886. In invoking Nietzsche's view of the autobiographical aspect of philosophy, I do not intend to be taken as endorsing his other philosophical positions.

3. René Descartes, *Meditations*, in *The Philosophical Writings of Descartes*, vol. II, trans. John Cottingham, Robert Stoothoff, and Dugald Murdoch (New York: Cambridge University Press, 1984), 13. Orig. pub. 1641.

4. Ibid.

5. As Claudia Card has pointed out to me, there was not even a body of *abstract* philosophical literature on rape, with the exception of Curley (1976), prior to the essays by Frederick Elliston, Carolyn M. Shafer and Marilyn Frye, Pamela Foa, and Susan Rae Peterson in Vetterling-Braggin et al. (1977). Also published in 1977 was Lorenne Clark and Debra Lewis, *Rape: The Price of Coercive Sexuality*. Now there are several anthologies of philosophical writings (with first-person narratives) on rape, including French et al. (1998), as well as a growing literature from other disciplines. See, for example, the first-person scholarship on rape by anthropologist Cathy Winkler, including "Rape as Social Murder."

6. See, for example, Diana Meyers, "Social Exclusion, Moral Reflection, and Rights," *Law and Philosophy* 12, no. 2 (May 1993), esp. 125–126.

7. Renato Rosaldo, *Culture and Truth: The Remaking of Social Analysis* (Boston: Beacon, 1989), 1–21.

8. Ibid., 3.

9. Ibid., 11.

10. For insightful discussions of the use of "we" in group identity politics, see Marianna Torgovnick, "The Politics of the 'We,'" in Torgovnick (1994, 260–277) and Brown (1995).

11. Huyssen (1995), 3. In addition, much recent psychological literature on memory stresses the construction that goes on in memory and argues against the "snapshot" (or "videotape" or "flashbulb") model of memory. See especially the debate about recovered memory therapy, including contributions by Ian Hacking (1995), Elizabeth Loftus and K. Ketcham (1994), and Lenore Terr (1994).

12. See Nelson Goodman, *Languages of Art* (Indianapolis: Hackett, 1976), 14–16.

13. Jonathan Culler, *Framing the Sign: Criticism and Its Institutions* (Norman: University of Oklahoma Press, 1988), xiv.

14. Another common example of "victim-talk" generating counter-"victim-talk" is in the area of domestic violence litigation in which *each* partner may claim to be *the* victim. I thank Claudia Card for mentioning this example.

15. For recent first-person narratives by feminist philosophers on some of these topics, see Wendell (1996—on living with a disability) and Kittay (1998—on caring for a disabled child).

16. Barbara Christian, "Remembering Audre Lorde," *Women's Review of Books* 10 (March 1993): 5.

T H R E E   Outliving Oneself

1. Delbo (1995, 267) attributes this statement to one of her fellow deportees.

2. Quoted in Langer (1995b, 14). The irony of calling the author of this quote a "survivor" is evident, but, it seems to me, linguistically unavoidable.

3. Shay (1994, 180). Shay writes, "When a survivor of prolonged trauma loses all sense of meaningful personal narrative, this may result in a contaminated identity. 'I died in Vietnam' may express a current identity as a corpse."

4. Scherer (1992, 179).

5. I do not mean to imply that the traumas suffered by these different groups of survivors are the same, or even commensurable. However, researchers such as Judith Herman, in *Trauma and Recovery* (1992), and Ronnie Janoff-Bulman, in *Shattered Assumptions: Towards a New Psychology of Trauma* (1992), have persuasively argued that many of those who survive life-threatening traumatic events in which they are reduced to near-complete helplessness later suffer from the symptoms of post-traumatic stress disorder. I would add that they experience a similar disintegration of the self. In this essay, I use the term "victim" as well as the term "survivor" to denote someone who has been victimized by, and yet survived, such a life-threatening trauma. Clearly, many civilians are more traumatized by war (and with greater injustice) than the veterans to whom I refer in this chapter. I mention the latter simply because trauma research on survivors of war has focused on veterans—U.S. veterans in particular—whose trauma symptoms our federal government is obliged to attempt to understand and treat.

6. In defending a feminist account of the relational self, I do not mean to imply that all relational accounts of the self are feminist. Some that are not (necessarily) feminist are those advocated by Hegel, Marx, and contemporary communitarians.

7. See Locke (1974, orig. pub. 1694), Noonan (1989), and Perry (1975) for treatments of personal identity by seventeenth- and eighteenth-century philosophers.

8. See Ungar (1990), Parfit (1986), Noonan (1989), Rorty (1976), and Perry (1975) for discussions of contemporary theories of personal identity.

9. While most philosophers writing about personal identity have neglected to consider *any* actual transformations of real persons, there are a few notable exceptions. Kathleen Wilkes argues that the "bizarre, entertaining, confusing, and inconclusive thought experiments" so common in philosophical writing about personal identity are not helpful, and, in any case, not needed, "since there are so many actual puzzle-cases which defy the *imagination*, but which we none the less have to accept as facts" (Wilkes 1988, vii). She does not discuss trauma, however, and uses third-person scientific accounts of neurological disorders rather than first person narratives in her analysis. Although he does not discuss trauma and the self either, Thomas Nagel examines the effect of commissurotomy on the self in "Brain Bisection and the Unity of Consciousness" (1975). Three philosophers, however, have in recent writings departed from this tradition of ignoring trauma and have analyzed alleged cases of trauma-induced dissociation and subsequent recovered memories. Ian Hacking (1995) presents a deeply skeptical treatment of the alleged splitting of the self that occurs during severe child abuse, while Naomi Scheman considers the multiple personalities constructed by severely abused children to be "a comprehensible, perhaps even rational, response to an intolerable situation, a way of maintaining some degree of agency in the face of profoundly soul-destroying attacks on one's ability to construct a sense of self" (1993, 164). Diana T. Meyers, in "The Family Romance" (Meyers, 1997, 440–457), mediates between these two views with an account focusing, not on whether the incest trope that "figures" such recovered memories is historically accurate, but, rather, on whether such a figuration is useful to the alleged victims.

10. For discussions of the usefulness of such narratives, see Brison (1995a) and Brison (1995b).

11. See King (1988), Lugones (1987), and Matsuda (1989).

12. This is not (merely) because philosophers are a more disputatious lot, but rather because psychologists need at least the appearance of clarity and agreement in order to categorize illnesses, make diagnoses, carry out research, fill out insurance claim forms, and so on.

13. This paraphrases Judith Herman's description of traumatic

events (1992, 33). This description and the following discussion of trauma are distilled from Herman's book as well as from Janoff-Bulman (1992) and Shay (1994).

14. While some poststructuralists hold that the self is a fiction, not all do, and this is not, in any case, implied by the view that it is a narrative. I think the clinical studies and narrative accounts of trauma discussed below show that the self is not a fiction, if that is taken to mean that it is freely constructed by some narrator. No one, not even Stephen King, would voluntarily construct a self so tormented by trauma and its aftermath.

15. Baier (1985, 84). For other discussions of the relational self, see Jaggar (1983) and Meyers (1987, 1989, 1992, 1994). Virginia Held gives an excellent survey of feminist views of the relational self in so far as they bear on moral theory (Held 1993, 57–64).

16. An exception is Bernard Williams (1970), who presents a thought experiment that prompts the intuition that in at least some cases of so-called body transfer, we would identify with the surviving individual who has our body, and not the one who has our memory and other psychological characteristics.

17. Most famously, Descartes (1984).

18. In refreshing contrast to this disciplinary bias is the philosophical writing on embodiment by Iris Young (1990).

19. Plato, *Phaedo*, II.65c–67d (quoted in Ruddick 1989, 188).

20. Two critiques of Beauvoir's position on maternity and childbirth are presented in Ruddick (1989, 192–193, 275, n. 11) and Mackenzie (1996).

21. Quoted in Ruddick (1989, 212).

22. That fear, anxiety, and so on are psychological, and hence controllable, responses to trauma is an assumption underlying the view, held by many liberals, that victims of hate speech should simply toughen their emotional hides to avoid being affected adversely by it. This view presupposes a mind-body split more thoroughgoing than that defended by Descartes (1984).

23. See also the discussion of charged memory in Proust in Glover (1988, 142–145).

24. If memories do not reside solely in the mind or in the body, but rather are a function of the way in which consciousness "inhabits" a body, then not only Locke's thought experiment, but also Sydney Shoemaker's (Perry 1975, 119–134) and Bernard Williams' (1970) appear to be incoherent as described.

25. And, in the case of the extreme trauma endured by Holocaust survivors, their bodies themselves were drastically changed, by starvation, disease, and torture.

26. An especially striking literary illustration of this is the scene in *Studs Lonigan* in which the narrator says of the woman Weary Reilly is about to rape, "She was his meat" (James T. Farrell, *Studs Lonigan*, Book II [New York: Vanguard, 1935], 396). I thank Blanche Gelfant for drawing my attention to this passage.

27. Ka-Tzetnik 135633 (1989). I thank Alexis Jetter for showing me the work of this author.

28. Nermina Zildzo, essay for English 2, Dartmouth College, Fall 1995.

29. See Terr (1994) for an account of different responses to one-time and ongoing traumas.

30. Kafka, Franz, "In the Penal Colony," in *The Penal Colony: Stories and Short Pieces*, trans. Willa and Edwin Muir (New York: Schocken, 1948), 191–227.

31. Parfit would not, however, agree with the relational account of the self I am defending here. In her comments on a draft of this chapter, Susan Dwyer wondered "how many people who have not suffered trauma have a clear sense of what it was like to be them at some earlier point in their lives." She guessed "not many," and suggested that this "explains a number of rituals we engage in, taking photographs of significant events, keeping a diary, marking anniversaries, valuing family (i.e., people who were there, too, who can tell you about your former self)."

32. Bruno Bettelheim discusses the "personality-disintegrating" effects of being in a German concentration camp (1979, 25). "Being subjected to living in an extreme situation somehow contaminates permanently the old life and the old personality. This suggests that a personality which did not protect the individual against landing in an extreme situation seems so deficient to the person that he feels in need of widespread restructuring" (1979, 123–124). In spite of this conviction, trauma survivors are forced to reacquire at least some of their earlier illusions if life is to continue to be livable.

33. Of course, not many rape survivors are fortunate enough to have such an experience with the criminal justice system, given the low rates of reporting, prosecuting, and conviction of rapists. I also had the advantage of having my assailant tried in a French court, in which the adversarial system is not practiced, so I was not cross-examined by the defense lawyer. In addition, since the facts of the

case were not in dispute and my assailant's only defense was an (ultimately unsuccessful) insanity plea, no one in the courtroom questioned my narrative of what happened.

34. I am not suggesting that for this reason the memories of trauma survivors are less reliable than others' memories. In the subsequent story, Yael Tamir did not have a false memory of actually having lived through the Holocaust. Rather, the cultural climate in which she was raised led her to respond instinctively to certain things (a shouting German voice at a train station) in ways characteristic of those who had actually been deported. In any case, since all narrative memory involves reconstruction, trauma survivors' narratives are no less likely to be accurate than anyone else's. (I thank Susan Dwyer for encouraging me to make this last point more explicit.)

35. Levi writes that "[a]t a distance of forty years, my tattoo has become a part of my body," which no longer taints his sense of self (1989, 119).

36. Judges, chapter 19, verses 26–28, which Mieke Bal mentions in Bal 1988b and discusses at length in Bal (1988a) and Bal (1991).

37. *Newsweek*, January 16, 1995, 54.

38. Milan Kundera, *The Book of Laughter and Forgetting* (New York: Knopf, 1980), 3. I thank Joan Bolker for reminding me of this quote, with which she begins her review (1995, 12) of Terr (1994). In this article Bolker also refers to "term limits on memory" which, she says, were what the U.S. electorate really voted for in the November 1994 elections (1995, 15).

39. For an example of an endorsement account of autonomy, see Frankfurt (1988, chs. 5 and 12).

40. Two of the most prominent proponents of what West calls "cultural feminism" (and others have called "difference feminism") are Carol Gilligan (1982) and Sara Ruddick (1989).

41. The best-known advocate of "radical" or "dominance" feminism is Catharine MacKinnon (1987).

42. The militaristic nature of this image is brought out by an update of this notion mentioned to me by Diana Meyers: autonomy as "the inner missile silo"!

43. In addition, not simply what we are able to express, but also what we are able to feel, can be seen to be a function of one's social relations. See Scheman (1983).

44. This is one of the positive aspects of a kind of multiple consciousness. Cf. Scheman (1993), Lugones (1987), Matsuda (1989), and King (1988).

45. Seeskin (1988, 120), quoting Emil Fackenheim, *To Mend the World* (New York: Schocken, 1982), 239.

46. When I later mentioned this to my therapist, she replied, reasonably enough, "Why not shoot the assailant instead?" But for me that thought was not yet thinkable.

47. I should make a distinction here between the ability to kill in self-defense and the desire to kill as a form of revenge. While I think it is morally permissible to possess and to employ the former, acting on the latter is to be morally condemned.

48. The idea that a child makes one twice as mortal comes from Barbara Kingsolver. A character in her story "Covered Bridges" says, "Having a child wouldn't make you immortal. It would make you twice as mortal. It's just one more life you could possibly lose, besides your own. Two more eyes to be put out, and ten more toes to get caught under the mower." Barbara Kingsolver, *Homeland and Other Stories* (New York: Harper & Row, 1989), 59–60.

49. Beckett (1965, 414). What Beckett actually writes is "you must go on, I can't go on, I'll go on," translating his original ending to *L'Innommable* (Paris: Minuit, 1953), 213: "*il faut continuer, je ne peux pas continuer, je vais continuer.*" I'm grateful to Thomas Trezise for pointing out this passage.

50. For a discussion of Pascal's wager, see Pascal (1958) and for William James' discussion of "the will to believe," see James (1896).

F O U R   Acts of Memory

1. Janet (1984, vol. 2, 272).

2. Dori Laub, "An Event Without a Witness: Truth, Testimony and Survival," in Felman and Laub (1992, 78).

3. Ibid.

4. See, for example, Sigmund Freud, "Remembering, Repeating and Working-Through," in *The Standard Edition of the Complete Psychological Works of Sigmund Freud* (hereafter cited as *SE*) vol. 12, 1958, 145–156, orig. pub. 1914; Freud, "Mourning and Melancholia," in *SE*, vol. 14, 1957, 238–258, orig. pub. 1917; Freud, *Beyond the Pleasure Principle*, in *SE*, vol. 18, 1955, 3–64, orig. pub. 1920; Janet, (1984).

5. My use of the term is influenced by the *DSM IV*, Judith Herman, Jonathan Shay, Bessel van der Kolk and Onno van der Hart, and others who talk about "trauma" in a wide range of groups. *DSM IV* (1994, 424–429); Herman (1992; Shay (1994); van der Kolk and van Der Hart, "The Intrusive Past: The Flexibility of Memory and the

Engraving of Trauma," in Caruth, ed. (1995, 158–182). The definition of "trauma" employed by those above includes trauma *not* of human origin. However, I am restricting my discussion to trauma of human origin since it affects the survivor's sense of self in a particular way, by leading to a sense of betrayal by—and inability to trust—one's fellow human beings.

In addition, my use of the word "trauma" is closer to Freud's implicit use of it in the term "traumatic neurosis" (defined, by Laplanche and Pontalis, as the "[t]ype of neurosis in which the appearance of symptoms follows upon an emotional shock generally associated with a situation where the subject has felt his life to be in danger") than it is to his use of the word "trauma (psychical)," defined, by Laplanche and Pontalis, as "[a]n event in the subject's life defined by its intensity, by the subject's incapacity to respond adequately, and by the upheaval and long-lasting effects that it brings about in the psychical organisation." Laplanche and Pontalis (1973, 470 ["traumatic neurosis"] and 465 ["trauma (psychical)"]).

What survivors of trauma have in common, on my account, is that they experienced utter helplessness in the face of overwhelming, life-threatening violence of human origin (e.g., child abuse, rape, war, torture, the Holocaust). The use of this definition poses a serious danger of overbreadth, however. Why include, in the same discussion, such radically different forms of trauma as, for example, surviving a single incident of rape and surviving the Holocaust? These events are not commensurable. The single rape is not as traumatic as, nor is it traumatic in the same ways as, the many horrific events experienced by individuals during the Holocaust. But there are similarities in what the survivors experience in the aftermath of violence, as well as similarities in the role narrative can play in the survivors' recovery.

6. See Caruth (1995). This is reminiscent of both Descartes' and Hume's accounts of how, given that we are in direct cognitive contact only with ideas, we are able to distinguish between veridical perceptions and mere imaginings. For Descartes, we can tell which perceptions are veridical by the criterion that we are unable to will them away (or will them to be different from what they are). Imaginings (which, for Descartes, are prototypically visual, iconic) are, in contrast, voluntarily conjured up and manipulated. According to Hume, it is the "force and vivacity" of ideas that marks their correspondence to reality (whatever reality might be for a phenomenalist). For a different critique of Caruth and van der Kolk and van der Hart, see Leys (2000).

7. Likewise, it isn't only traumatic events that exceed our ability to describe them. At the edge of reason lies not only immobilizing terror, but also passionate, immoderate desire.

8. There seems to be a mind-body dualism underlying this, in which bodily memories are more reliable and stable, because they're unworked over by the consciousness. But I have been arguing that the study of trauma undermines mind-body dualism and that what gets lodged in the body in trauma is permeated with meaning. Furthermore, even if we were to accept a mind-body dualism, there would seem to be no reason to suppose that the body is a more reliable recorder of events than the mind. (Think of Descartes' and other philosophers' discussions of the ways the body deceives us, by subjecting us to sensory illusions, for example.)

9. This theory of trauma comes dangerously close to Arlene Croce's view of so-called victim art (Croce 1994/95). (See also Spelman's critique of Croce [Spelman 1997, 133–156].) Actually, it goes further: not only can there be no morally defensible aesthetic judgment of the art of survival, but the artwork itself is morally suspect, to the very extent that it manages to convey anything intelligible. For an analysis of this position, see Trezise (forthcoming 2001).

10. Austin (1962, 5). This claim is controversial, however. One might argue that some performative utterances, for example, "I do," *do* describe something and may be taken to be true or false.

11. This controversial conjecture is relevant to discussions of the collison between the roles of testimony in clinical settings and in courts of law in the "recovered memory" debate. Some analyses of so-called recovered memories emphasize the cultural pressures on certain individuals to "remember" things that may not have occurred (Hacking 1995; Sturken, "Recovered Memory Syndrome as Cultural Memory"; in Bal et al., eds., *Acts of Memory*, 231–248). Such pressures exist and, in addition, trauma survivors may be urged, in a particular cultural climate, to remember and testify to traumas that, in other cultural climates, they would be urged to forget. For example, the testimonies of women raped by the enemy in wartime are *sometimes* encouraged and used as propaganda against the enemy, whereas women raped on the home front by those not considered the enemy typically experience being silenced by their culture. (See Grossman 1997 for a fascinating discussion of the use of accounts of rape of German women by Soviet troops as cultural propaganda serving the Germans' self-characterization as "victims" of World War II.)

These phenomena should not obscure, however, the enormous pressure—both internal and external—exerted on trauma survivors to forget. Although it is beyond the scope of this book to discuss the current controversy over recovered memories, my discussion of the difficulties involved in testifying to trauma, including those of the listener, is pertinent to that controversy. Anecdotally, I can report that for many months following my assault—one for which there was considerable physical evidence as well as corroboration from others, including the perpetrator—I awoke each morning thinking, "This can't possibly have happened to me."

12. Laub, "An Event Without a Witness: Truth, Testimony and Survival," in Felman and Laub (1992, 86–87).

13. See, for example, Herman (1992, 33). As Herman notes, the trauma victim "is rendered helpless by overwhelming force. . . . Traumatic events overwhelm the ordinary systems of care that give people a sense of control, connection, and meaning."

14. It is important to recognize that survivors do not all employ the same strategies to regain control. For example, as Michele Fine has pointed out, disempowered persons may refrain from taking control by going to the police or seeking the help of a social worker, since they may have reasons to doubt the efficacy of such approaches. As Fine observes, "[t]aking control is undoubtedly a significant psychological experience; knowing that one can effect change in one's environment makes a difference. How individuals accomplish this, however, does vary by economic and social circumstance, gender, and perhaps personal style." Michele Fine, "Coping with Rape: Critical Perspectives on Consciousness," in Fine (1992, 73). From my readings, and from my experiences, including participation in a racially and economically diverse rape survivors' support group (at Women Organized against Rape, in Philadelphia), I have gathered that the attempt to regain control by means of self-blame is common to many survivors of different races and classes.

15. At the same time, the fact that victims (especially rape victims) so readily blame themselves for what happened is another reason for not taking victims' narrative at face value.

16. For an extensive discussion of this, see Melvin J. Lerner (1980).

17. A striking example of this is the study done by Rubin and Peplau of fifty-eight draft-eligible young men who were informed by the 1971 lottery of their likelihood of being drafted into the armed forces. They completed questionnaires designed to measure self-

esteem, both before and after hearing the results of the lottery. Those with bad draft rankings showed lowered self-esteem, while those with good ones showed enhanced self-esteem. This study is discussed in ibid., 140. Of course, depression can also lower self-esteem, and the subjects with bad luck were probably instantly depressed by the news.

18. These observations led me to speculate (in chapter 1) that experiencing anger toward one's attacker is so difficult because it requires imagining oneself in proximity to him, a prospect that is too terrifying if one is still feeling powerless with respect to him.

19. Dale T. Miller and Carol A. Porter (1983, 150) suggest that this splitting of the self may be one way of coping.

20. Patricia A. Resick notes that "two studies have found that rape victims who appraised the situation as 'safe' prior to the assault had greater fear and depressive reactions than women who perceived themselves to be in a dangerous situation prior to the assault (Frank & Stewart, 1984; Scheppele & Bart, 1983)." *Journal of Interpersonal Violence* (June 1993) 239. If there was nothing victims could have done to prevent the attack, such as avoiding certain dangerous settings or situations, there is nothing they could do to prevent a similar attack in the future. (The complete references to the articles cited by Resick are E. Frank and B. D. Stewart, "Depressive Symptoms in Rape Victims: A Revisit," *Journal of Affective Disorders* 1 [1984]: 77–85; K. L. Scheppele and P. B. Bart, "Through Women's Eyes: Defining Danger in the Wake of Sexual Assault," *Journal of Social Issues* 39 [1983]: 63–81.)

21. See Freud, *Beyond the Pleasure Principle*, in *SE*, vol. 18, 31–33, for a psychoanalytic account of this phenomenon.

22. See Bart and O'Brien (1984, 83–101).

23. One group of researchers who studied women students who took a self-defense class "saw them discover that feeling angry was an alternative to feeling fearful or helpless. Learning to become angry with someone else rather than feeling frightened or helpless may enable the students to assume responsibility for the solution without blaming themselves for the problem." Kidder et al. (1983, 167).

24. As C. H. Sparks and Bat-Ami Bar On have argued, self-defense tactics are "stop gap measures which fail to link an attack against one victim with attacks on others." And, as they point out, "[k]nowledge that one can fight if attacked is also a very different kind of security from enjoying a certainty that one will not be attacked at all." C. H. Sparks and B. A. Bar On, "A Social Change Approach to the Prevention of Sexual Violence against Women,"

Stone Center for Developmental Services and Studies, *Work in Progress*, series no. 83–08 (Wellesley, Mass.: Wellesley College, Stone Center for Developmental Services and Studies, 1985), 3.

25. Adrienne Rich, "Letters to a Young Poet," in *Midnight Salvage: Poems 1995–1998* (New York: W. W. Norton, 1999), 25.

26. *New York Times*, October 26, 1999, F1.

27. This may be a version of what Jon Elster describes as "adaptive preference formation" in Jon Elser, *Sour Grapes* (New York: Cambridge University Press, 1983).

F I V E   The Politics of Forgetting

1. Bertolt Brecht, *Poems 1913–1956*, ed. John Willett and Ralph Manheim (New York: Methuen, 1976), 247.

2. Marianne Hirsch (1997) and "Projected Memory: Holocaust Photographs in Personal and Public Fantasy," in Bal et al. (1999; 3–23). Hirsch uses the term "postmemory" to describe the relationship of children of survivors of cultural or collective trauma to the experiences of their parents, "experiences that they 'remember' only as the stories and images with which they grew up, but that are so powerful, so monumental, as to constitute memories in their own right." "Projected Memory," 8.

3. www.CNN.com, May 14, 1999.

4. Pierre Nora describes *les lieux de mémoire* as "enveloped in a Möbius strip of the collective and the individual." Nora (1989, 19). I adapt Nora's metaphor here to suggest that women's postmemories of rape are, paradoxically, enveloped in a Möbius strip merging past and future. This is not the only paradoxical aspect of the postmemory of rape. Somehow, women's sense of the naturalness, ubiquitousness, almost inevitability, of rape is combined with the contradictory attitude of "it could never happen to me."

5. I am not advocating this appropriation of others' trauma narratives and I am aware of the risk of misappropriation, especially of the Holocaust archetype. (For an insightful discussion of the misappropriation of Holocaust narratives, see James E. Young [1988 esp. 83–133].) But it is inevitable that events are experienced and later narrated through available archetypes. These, then, must be subjected to critical analysis.

6. At some point after getting a letter from Tom thanking him for his expert assistance, the chief of police who handled the case replied that he had done nothing particularly praiseworthy, that he was simply acting out of his *honneur d'homme*.

7. There is something infantilizing about being a victim of violence, and young women more neatly fit the stereotype of a rape victim. The newspaper report of my assailant's trial described me as a "young tourist" and Tom, who also testified at the trial, as "an eminent professor at one of the most prestigious universities in the U.S.," even though we were both, by that time, in our late thirties and, I hope I'll be forgiven for saying so, equally uneminent. Perhaps the newspaper emphasized Tom's status to show just whose interests were at stake in this trial, to highlight the class difference between the victim (the wife of an eminent professor) and the defendant (a poor farmer). This kind of class difference makes for a more "newsworthy" rape. See Helen Benedict (1992).

8. In a civil suit, I was awarded a small amount of money to cover some unreimbursed medical bills, legal expenses, and lost income.

9. The terms "*gentil*" and "*méchant*" could also be translated "nice" and "naughty," but I think the principle of charity in translation dictates my choice of English adjectives.

10. But, in a way, no description can completely do justice to the experience—or to its memory. As Charlotte Delbo writes, in the voice of Mado, of telling a narrative about surviving the Holocaust: "The very fact we're here to speak denies what we have to say" (1995, 257). This is not just because those narrating trauma are trying to get their listeners to believe the incredible, but also because, as Delbo writes, "None of us was meant to return" (114).

11. Described by Myrna Kostash in "Second Thoughts," in Varda Burstyn, ed., *Women Against Censorship* (Vancouver: Douglas & McIntyre, 1985), 38.

12. Verses include:

1. Oh Willy, Oh Willy, I fear for your way(s?) [2x]
   I fear you will lead my poor body astray.
2. Oh Polly, pretty Polly, you guessed about right [2x]
   I dug on your grave the best part of last night.
3. I stabbed her to the heart and her heart's blood did flow [2x]
   And into her grave Pretty Polly did go.
4. I throwed a little dirt o'er her and started for home [2x]
   Leaving nothing else behind but the wild birds to moan.

13. "Run For Your Life" (Lennon/McCartney) on "Rubber Soul." First issued December 3, 1965—Parlophone PMC 1267 (mono)—Parlophone PCS 3075 (stereo).

14. Broadcast on April 21, 1999. Reported in the *Rocky Mountain News* on April 24, 1999.

15. Sunday *New York Times* Book Review, August 15, 1993.

16. Susan Brownmiller (1975) was one of the best-known proponents of this view.

17. To the extent that we say anything about ourselves, we are using language to categorize ourselves as members of groups. If there are such things as "bare particulars" (particular entities without properties), we cannot speak of them.

18. See Brown (1995, 52–76).

19. For an excellent defense of the opposing view—that rape is a form of collective violence against women—see Claudia Card (1991).

20. Pamela Ballinger, "The Culture of Survivors: Post-Traumatic Stress Disorder and Traumatic Memory," *History and Memory* 10, no. 1 (Spring 1988): 121–122.

21. Bertolt Brecht, *Poems: 1913–1956*, ed. John Willett and Ralph Manheim (New York: Methuen, 1976), 247.

22. For accounts of the harmful effects of "untold stories" on children of survivors of the Holocaust, see Fresco (1984) and Bar-On (1995).

S I X   Retellings

1. Samuel Beckett, *Stories and Texts for Nothing* (New York: Grove, 1967), 85, 77.

2. Aristotle, "Poetics" in Aristotle (1984, 2321).

3. Barbara Herrnstein Smith, "Afterthoughts on Narrative," in *On Narrative*, ed. W.J.T. Mitchell (Chicago: University of Chicago Press, 1981), 228. Since I think narratives can be told to oneself, intrapsychically, I would not, however, stress, as Smith does, that a narrative must be told to "*someone else.*"

4. See, for example, the definitions of "surd" in *The American Heritage Dictionary of the English Language*, 4th ed. (New York: Houghton Mifflin, 2000).

5. Caruth (1995, 1996) and van der Hart and van der Kolk in Caruth (1996) take the involuntariness of traumatic memories to be evidence for their "literality," but it is not clear why. Perhaps it is because, on their account, trauma is not consciously experienced. This view, combined with the (I think, implausible) assumption that only what is conscious is worked over by the mind, could lead to the (I think, false) conclusion that traumatic memories are objective, timeless, and accurate recordings of the traumatic event itself.

6. See Ziegenmeyer (1992), Scherer (1992), Raine (1998), and Francisco (1999). That all of these rape memoirs were written by

fairly well-off white women (with backgrounds that were privileged emotionally, as well as educationally and financially) goes a long way toward explaining the trajectory of what I'm calling the "expected plot."

7. Judith Lewis Herman, *Trauma and Recovery* (New York: Basic, 1992), 57.

8. Only two rape narratives that I've read share this feature—Jamie Kalven's *Working with Available Light* and Alice Sebold's *Lucky*. Sebold recounts the aftermath of her rape in a straightforward, jargon-free way—in part, perhaps, because she encountered the professional psychological research on trauma only after having written much of her book. (She writes about having discovered Herman's *Trauma and Recovery* only *after* she had written about her own assault in the *Sunday New York Times Magazine*.) She doesn't write about her recovery in terms of the neat phases of denial, anger, and integration that often appear in rape memoirs and she never idealizes a pre-rape past or mourns a time of blissful innocence. She acknowledges that life can be hard, in various ways, both before and after a rape.

9. These lines are from "Invictus" by William Ernest Henley.

10. This phrase comes from May Sarton's poem "Night Watch" in her *Collected Poems (1930–1973)* (New York: W. W. Norton, 1974), 326. She writes of feeling "pain like an assault" and having "to decide / To be crazy-human with hope / Or just plain crazy / With fear."

11. Ludwig Wittgenstein, *Culture and Value*, ed. G. H. Von Wright, trans. Peter Winch (Chicago: University of Chicago Press, 1980), 1e. My translation differs slightly from Winch's.

Afterword

1. From Rainer Maria Rilke, *The Sonnets to Orpheus*, II, 13, in *The Selected Poetry of Rainer Maria Rilke*, ed. and trans. Stephen Mitchell (New York: Random House, 1982), 245.

2. From May Sarton, "All Souls," in her *Collected Poems (1930–1973)* (New York: W. W. Norton, 1974), 185.

Acknowledgments

1. From "One Art," in Elizabeth Bishop, *The Complete Poems: 1927–1979* (New York: Farrar, Straus and Giroux, 1979), 178.

Bibliography

Alcoff, Linda, and Laura Gray. 1993. "Survivor Discourse: Transgression or Recuperation?" *Signs: Journal of Women in Culture and Society* 18: 83–101.

Améry, Jean. 1995. "Torture." In *Art from the Ashes: A Holocaust Anthology*, ed. Lawrence Langer. New York: Oxford University Press.

Aristotle. 1984. *The Complete Works of Aristotle*. Vol. 2. Ed. Jonathan Barnes. Princeton: Princeton University Press.

Austin, J. L. 1962. *How to Do Things with Words*. Cambridge, Mass.: Harvard University Press.

Baier, Annette. 1985. *Postures of the Mind: Essays on Mind and Morals*. Minneapolis: University of Minnesota Press.

———. 1994. *Moral Prejudices: Essays on Ethics*. Cambridge, Mass.: Harvard University Press.

Bal, Mieke. 1988a. *Death and Dissymmetry: The Politics of Coherence in the Book of Judges*. Chicago: University of Chicago Press.

———. 1988b. *Murder and Difference: Gender, Genre, and Scholarship on Sisera's Death.* Bloomington: Indiana University Press.

———. 1991. *Reading "Rembrandt": Beyond the Word-Image Opposition.* New York: Cambridge University Press.

Bal, Mieke, Jonathan Crewe, and Leo Spitzer, eds. 1999. *Acts of Memory: Cultural Recall in the Present.* Hanover: University Press of New England.

Ballinger, Pamela. 1998. "The Culture of Survivors: Post-Traumatic Stress Disorder and Traumatic Memory." *History and Memory* 10, no. 1.

Bard, Morton, and Dawn Sangrey. 1986. *The Crime Victim's Book.* New York: Brunner/Mazel.

Bar-On, Dan. 1995. *Fear and Hope: Three Generations of the Holocaust.* Cambridge, Mass.: Harvard University Press.

Bart, Pauline B., and Patricia H. O'Brien. 1984. "Stopping Rape: Effective Avoidance Strategies." *Signs: Journal of Women in Culture and Society* 10, no. 1: 83–101.

Beauvoir, Simone de. 1953. *The Second Sex.* Trans. H. M. Parshley. New York: Vintage.

Beckett, Samuel. 1965. *Three Novels.* New York: Grove.

Benedict, Helen. 1985. *Recovery: How to Survive Sexual Assault—for Women, Men, Teenagers, Their Friends and Families.* Garden City, N.Y.: Doubleday.

———. 1992. *Virgin or Vamp: How the Press Covers Sex Crimes.* New York: Oxford University Press.

Bettelheim, Bruno. 1979. *Surviving and Other Essays.* New York: Knopf.

Bolker, Joan L. 1995. "Forgetting Ourselves." *Readings: A Journal of Reviews and Commentary in Mental Health,* June: 12–15.

Braidotti, Rosi. 1994. *Nomadic Subjects: Embodiment and Sexual Difference in Contemporary Feminist Theory.* New York: Columbia University Press.

Brison, Susan. 1993. "Surviving Sexual Violence: A Philosophical Perspective." *Journal of Social Philosophy* 24, no. 1: 5–22.

———. 1995a. "The Theoretical Importance of Practice." *Nomos* 37: 216–238.

———. 1995b. "On the Personal as Philosophical." *APA Newsletter* 95, no. 1: 37–40.

———. 1998. "Speech, Harm, and the Mind-Body Problem in First Amendment Jurisprudence." *Legal Theory* 4: 39–61.

Brown, Wendy. 1995. *States of Injury*. Princeton: Princeton University Press.

Brownmiller, Susan. 1975. *Against Our Will: Men, Women, and Rape*. New York: Bantam.

Card, Claudia. 1991. "Rape as a Terrorist Institution." In *Violence, Terrorism, and Justice*, ed. R. G. Frey and Christopher W. Morris, 296–319. Cambridge: Cambridge University Press.

Caruth, Cathy, ed. 1995. *Trauma: Explorations in Memory*. Baltimore: Johns Hopkins University Press.

———. 1996. *Unclaimed Experience: Trauma, Narrative, and History*. Baltimore: Johns Hopkins University Press.

Clark, Lorenne, and Debra Lewis. 1977. *Rape: The Price of Coercive Sexuality*. Toronto: The Women's Press.

Croce, Arlene. 1994–95. "Discussing the Undiscussable." *The New Yorker*. December 24, 1994/January 2, 1995, 54–60.

Culbertson, Roberta. 1995. "Embodied Memory, Transcendence, and Telling: Recounting Trauma, Re-establishing the Self." *New Literary History* 26: 169–195.

Curley, E. M. 1976. "Excusing Rape." *Philosophy & Public Affairs* 5: 325–360.

Delbo, Charlotte. 1985. *Days and Memory*. Trans. Rosette Lamont. Marlboro, Vt.: The Marlboro Press.

———. 1995. *Auschwitz and After*. Trans. Rosette C. Lamont. New Haven: Yale University Press.

Descartes, René. 1984 (orig. pub. 1641). *Meditations*. In *The Philosophical Writings of Descartes*, vol. II, trans. John Cottingham, Robert Stoothoff, and Dugald Murdoch. New York: Cambridge University Press.

de Sousa, Ronald. 1987. *The Rationality of Emotion*. Cambridge, Mass.: The MIT Press.

DSM IV. 1994. *Diagnostic and Statistical Manual of Mental Disorders*. 4th ed. Washington, D.C.: American Psychiatric Association.

Estrich, Susan. 1987. *Real Rape*. Cambridge, Mass.: Harvard University Press.

Felman, Shoshana, and Dori Laub, eds. 1992. *Testimony: Crises of Witnessing in Literature, Psychoanalysis, and History*. New York: Routledge.

Fine, Michele. 1992. *Disruptive Voices*. Ann Arbor: University of Michigan Press.

Francisco, Patricia Weaver. 1999. *Telling: A Memoir of Rape and Recovery*. New York: HarperCollins.

Frankfurt, Harry. 1988. *The Importance of What We Care About.* New York: Cambridge University Press.

French, Stanley, Laura Purdy, and Wanda Teays, eds. 1998. *Philosophical Perspectives on Violence against Women.* Ithaca, N.Y.: Cornell University Press.

Fresco, Nadine. 1984. "Remembering the Unknown." *International Review of Psychoanalysis* 11: 417–427.

Freud, Sigmund. 1953–74. *The Standard Edition of the Complete Psychological Works of Sigmund Freud (SE).* Trans. under the general editorship of James Strachey in collaboration with Anna Freud, assisted by Alix Strachey and Alan Tyson. 24 vols. London: Hogarth.

Fussell, Paul. 1975. *The Great War and Modern Memory.* New York: Oxford University Press.

Gilligan, Carol. 1982. *In a Different Voice.* Cambridge, Mass.: Harvard University Press.

Glover, Jonathan. 1988. *I: The Philosophy and Psychology of Personal Identity.* London: Allen Lane, Penguin.

Gordon, Margaret T., and Stephanie Riger. 1991. *The Female Fear: The Social Cost of Rape.* Chicago: University of Illinois Press.

Grossman, Anita. 1997. "A Question of Silence: The Rape of German Women by Occupation Soldiers." In *West Germany Under Construction: Politics, Society, and Culture in the Adenauer Era,* ed. Robert G. Moeller, 33–52. Ann Arbor: University of Michigan Press.

Hacking, Ian. 1995. *Rewriting the Soul: Multiple Personality and the Sciences of Memory.* Princeton: Princeton University Press.

Halbwachs, Maurice. 1992 (orig. pub. 1941 and 1952). *On Collective Memory.* Ed. and trans. Lewis A. Coser. Chicago: University of Chicago Press.

Harrison, Ross. 1986. "Rape Case Study in Political Philosophy." In *Rape: An Historical and Cultural Enquiry,* ed. Sylvana Tomaselli and Roy Porter, 41–56. New York: Basil Blackwell.

Held, Virginia. 1993. *Feminist Morality: Transforming Culture, Society, and Politics.* Chicago: University of Chicago Press.

Herman, Judith Lewis. 1992. *Trauma and Recovery.* New York: Basic.

Hirsch, Marianne. 1992–93. "Family Pictures: *Maus,* Mourning, and Post-Memory." *Discourse* 15, no. 2: 3–29.

———. 1997. *Family Frames: Photography, Narrative, and Postmemory.* Cambridge, Mass.: Harvard University Press.

Hoffman, Eva. 1989. *Lost in Translation.* New York: Dutton.

Huyssen, Andreas. 1995. *Twilight Memories: Marking Time in a Culture of Amnesia.* New York: Routledge.

Jaggar, Alison M. 1983. *Feminist Politics and Human Nature.* Totowa, N.J.: Rowman & Allanheld.

James, William. 1896. *The Will to Believe and Other Essays in Popular Philosophy.* New York: Longmans, Green.

Janet, Pierre. 1984 (orig. pub. 1919–25). *Les médications psychologiques.* 3 vols. Paris: Société Pierre Janet.

Janoff-Bulman, Ronnie. 1979. "Characterological versus Behavioral Self-Blame: Inquiries into Depression and Rape." *Journal of Personality and Social Psychology* 37, no. 10: 1798–1809.

———. 1992. *Shattered Assumptions: Towards a New Psychology of Trauma.* New York: The Free Press.

Kalven, Jamie. 1999. *Working with Available Light: A Family's World after Violence.* New York: W. W. Norton.

Ka-Tzetnik 135633. 1989. *Shivitti: A Vision.* New York: Harper & Row.

Kidder, Louise H. , Joanne L. Boell, and Marilyn M. Moyer. 1983. "Rights Consciousness and Victimization Prevention: Personal Defense and Assertiveness Training." *Journal of Social Issues* 39, no. 2.

King, Deborah K. 1988. "Multiple Jeopardy, Multiple Consciousness: The Context of a Black Feminist Ideology." *Signs* 14, no. 1: 42–72.

Kittay, Eva. 1998. *Love's Labor: Essays on Women, Equality and Dependency.* New York: Routledge.

Kittay, Eva Feder, and Diana Tietjens Meyers, eds. 1987. *Women and Moral Theory.* Savage, Md.: Rowman and Littlefield.

Koss, Mary P., and Mary R. Harvey. 1991. *The Rape Victim: Clinical and Community Interventions.* 2nd ed. London: Sage.

Kramer, Peter. 1993. *Listening to Prozac.* New York: Viking.

LaCapra, Dominick. 1994. *Representing the Holocaust: History, Theory, Trauma.* Ithaca: Cornell University Press.

———. 1998. *History and Memory after Auschwitz.* Ithaca: Cornell University Press.

Lamb, Sharon, ed. 1999. *New Versions of Victims: Feminists Struggle with the Concept.* New York: New York University Press.

———. 1996. *The Trouble with Blame: Victims, Perpetrators, and Responsibility.* Cambridge, Mass.: Harvard University Press.

Langer, Lawrence. 1995a. *Admitting the Holocaust.* New York: Oxford University Press.

————, ed. 1995b. *Art from the Ashes*. New York: Oxford University Press.

Laplanche, J., and J.-B. Pontalis. 1973. *The Language of Psychoanalysis*. Trans. Donald Nicholson-Smith. New York: W. W. Norton.

Lawrence, Charles R., III. 1990. "If He Hollers Let Him Go: Regulating Racist Speech on Campus." *Duke Law Journal* 1990: 431–483.

Le Guin, Ursula. 1989. *Dancing at the Edge of the World: Thoughts on Words, Women, Places*. New York: Grove.

Lerner, Melvin J. 1980. *The Belief in a Just World: A Fundamental Delusion*. New York: Plenum.

Levi, Primo. 1985. *If Not Now, When?* New York: Penguin.

————. 1989. *The Drowned and the Saved*. New York: Random House.

————. 1993. *Survival in Auschwitz*. New York: Macmillan.

Levinas, Emmanuel. 1996. *Proper Names*. Stanford: Stanford University Press.

Leys, Ruth. 2000. *Trauma: A Genealogy*. Chicago: University of Chicago Press.

Locke, John. 1974. (This section, on personal identity, was orig. pub. 1694.) *An Essay Concerning Human Understanding*, ed. A. D. Woozley, 210–220. New York: New American Library.

Loftus, Elizabeth, and K. Ketcham. 1994. *The Myth of Repressed Memories: False Memories and Allegations of Sexual Abuse*. New York: St. Martin's.

Lugones, Maria. 1987. "Playfulness, 'World'-Travelling, and Loving Perception." *Hypatia* 2, no. 2: 3–19.

Mackenzie, Catriona. 1996. "A Certain Lack of Symmetry: de Beauvoir on Autonomous Agency and Women's Embodiment." In *Texts in Culture: Simone de Beauvoir, "The Second Sex,"* ed. Ruth Evans. Manchester: Manchester University Press.

MacKinnon, Catharine. 1987. *Feminism Unmodified: Discourses on Life and Law*. Cambridge, Mass.: Harvard University Press.

————. 1993. *Only Words*. Cambridge, Mass.: Harvard University Press.

Matsuda, Mari. 1989a. "Public Response to Racist Speech: Considering the Victim's Story." *Michigan Law Review* 87, no. 8: 2320–2381.

————. 1989b. "When the First Quail Calls: Multiple Consciousness as Jurisprudential Method." *Women's Rights Law Reporter* 11, no. 1: 7–10.

Meyers, Diana Tietjens. 1986. "The Politics of Self-Respect: A Feminist Perspective." *Hypatia* 1, no. 1: 83–100.

———. 1987. "The Socialized Individual and Individual Autonomy: An Intersection between Philosophy and Psychology." In *Women and Moral Theory*, ed. Eva Feder Kittay and Diana Tietjens Meyers. Savage, Md.: Rowman and Littlefield.

———. 1989. *Self, Society, and Personal Choice.* New York: Columbia University Press.

———. 1992. "Personal Autonomy or the Deconstructed Subject? A Reply to Hekman." *Hypatia* 7, no. 1: 124–132.

———. 1994. *Subjection & Subjectivity: Psychoanalytic Feminism & Moral Philosophy.* New York: Routledge.

———. ed. 1997. *Feminist Social Thought: A Reader.* New York: Routledge.

Miedzian, Myriam. 1991. *Boys Will Be Boys: Breaking the Link between Masculinity and Violence.* New York: Doubleday.

Miller, Dale T., and Carol A. Porter. 1983. "Self-Blame in Victims of Violence." *Journal of Social Issues* 39, no. 2.

Minow, Martha. 1990. *Making All the Difference: Inclusion, Exclusion, and American Law.* Ithaca: Cornell University Press.

———. 1993. "Surviving Victim Talk." *UCLA Law Review* 40.

Mitchell, Juliet. 2000. *Mad Men and Medusas: Reclaiming Hysteria.* New York: Basic.

Mitchell, W. J. T., ed. 1981. *On Narrative.* Chicago: University of Chicago Press.

Nagel, Thomas. 1975. "Brain Bisection and the Unity of Consciousness." In *Personal Identity*, ed. John Perry. Berkeley: University of California Press.

Nedelsky, Jennifer. 1989. "Reconceiving Autonomy: Sources, Thoughts and Possibilities." *Yale Journal of Law and Feminism* 1, no. 7: 7–36.

Noddings, Nell. 1989. *Women and Evil.* Berkeley: University of California Press.

Noonan, Harold W. 1989. *Personal Identity.* New York: Routledge.

Nora, Pierre. 1989. "Between History and Memory: Les Lieux de Mémoire," *Representations* 26.

Nozick, Robert. 1989. The *Examined Life: Philosophical Meditations.* New York: Touchstone.

Parfit, Derek. 1986. *Reasons and Persons.* Oxford: Oxford University Press.

Pascal, Blaise. 1958. *Pensées.* Trans. W. F. Trotter. New York: Dutton.

Perry, John. 1975. *Personal Identity*. Berkeley: University of California Press.

Pierce-Baker, Charlotte. 1998. *Surviving the Silence: Black Women's Stories of Rape*. New York: W. W. Norton.

Pineau, Lois. 1989. "Date Rape: A Feminist Analysis." *Law and Philosophy* 8: 217–243.

Proust, Marcel. 1981. *Remembrance of Things Past*. Trans. C. K. Scott Moncrieff and Terence Kilmartin. New York: Vintage.

Raine, Nancy Venable. 1998. *After Silence: Rape and My Journey Back*. New York: Crown.

Rawls, John. 1971. *A Theory of Justice*. Cambridge, Mass.: Harvard University Press.

Roberts, Cathy. 1989. *Women and Rape*. New York: New York University Press.

Rorty, Amélie Oksenberg, ed. 1976. *The Identities of Persons*. Berkeley: University of California Press.

Ruddick, Sara. 1989. *Maternal Thinking: Toward a Politics of Peace*. Boston: Beacon.

Russell, Diana E. H., and Nancy Howell. 1983. "The Prevalence of Rape in the United States Revisited." *Signs: Journal of Women in Culture and Society* 8, no. 4: 68–95.

Scheman, Naomi. 1983. "Individualism and the Objects of Psychology." In *Discovering Reality: Feminist Perspectives on Epistemology, Metaphysics, Methodology, and Philosophy of Science*, ed. Sandra Harding and Merrill B. Hintikka, 225–244. Boston: D. Reidel.

———. 1993. "Though This Be Method, Yet There Is Madness in It." In *A Mind of One's Own*, ed. Louise M. Antony and Charlotte Witt. Boulder, Colo.: Westview.

Scherer, Migael. 1992. *Still Loved by the Sun: A Rape Survivor's Journal*. New York: Simon & Schuster.

Scott, Joan W. 1992. "'Experience.'" In *Feminists Theorize the Political*, ed. Judith Butler and Joan W. Scott, 22–40. New York: Routledge.

Sebold, Alice. 1999. *Lucky*. New York: Scribner.

Seeskin, Kenneth. 1988. "Coming to Terms with Failure: A Philosophical Dilemma." In *Writing and the Holocaust*, ed. Berel Lang. New York: Holmes & Meier.

Segev, Tom. 1993. *The Seventh Million*. Trans. Haim Watzman. New York: Hill and Wang.

Shay, Jonathan. 1994. *Achilles in Vietnam: Combat Trauma and the Undoing of Character*. New York: Atheneum.

Silverman, Kaja. 1996. *The Threshold of the Visible World*. New York: Routledge.

Spelman, Elizabeth V. 1997. *Fruits of Sorrow: Framing Our Attention to Suffering*. Boston: Beacon.

Sturken, Marita. 1997. *Tangled Memories: The Vietnam War, the AIDS Epidemic, and the Politics of Remembering*. Berkeley and Los Angeles: University of California Press.

Terr, Lenore. 1994. *Unchained Memories*. New York: HarperCollins.

Tonkin, Elizabeth. 1992. *Narrating Our Pasts: The Social Construction of Oral History*. New York: Cambridge University Press.

Torgovnick, Marianna, ed. 1994. *Eloquent Obsessions: Writing Cultural Criticism*. Durham: Duke University Press.

Trezise, Thomas A. Forthcoming 2001. "Unspeakable." *The Yale Journal of Criticism*. Special Issue on the Holocaust and Criticism.

Ungar, Peter. 1990. *Identity, Consciousness and Value*. New York: Oxford University Press.

Vetterling-Braggin, Mary, Frederick Elliston, and Jane English, eds. 1977. *Feminism and Philosophy*. Totowa, N.J.: Littlefield, Adams.

Warshaw, Robin. 1988. *I Never Called It Rape*. New York: Harper & Row.

Wendell, Susan. 1996. *The Rejected Body: Feminist Philosophical Reflections on Disability*. New York: Routledge.

West, Robin. 1988. "Jurisprudence and Gender." *University of Chicago Law Review* 55, no. 6: 1–72.

Wiesel, Elie. 1990 (orig. pub. 1960). *The Night Trilogy*. New York: Hill and Wang.

Wilkes, Kathleen. 1988. *Real People*. New York: Oxford University Press.

Williams, Bernard. 1970. "The Self and the Future." *Philosophical Review* 79, no. 2: 161–180.

Williams, Patricia J. 1991. *The Alchemy of Race and Rights*. Cambridge, Mass.: Harvard University Press.

———. 1995. *The Rooster's Egg: On the Persistence of Prejudice*. Cambridge, Mass.: Harvard University Press.

———. 1997. *Seeing a Colour-Blind Future: The Paradox of Race*. London: Virago.

Winkler, Cathy. 1991. "Rape as Social Murder." *Anthropology Today* 7, no. 3: 12–14.

———. Forthcoming 2002. *One Night: Realities of Rape*. Walnut Creek, Calif.: Altamira.

Young, Iris Marion. 1990. *Throwing Like a Girl and Other Essays in*

Feminist Philosophy and Social Theory. Indianapolis: Indiana University Press.

Young, James E. 1988. *Writing and Rewriting the Holocaust: Narrative and the Consequences of Interpretation.* Bloomington: Indiana University Press, 1988.

Ziegenmeyer, Nancy. 1992. *Taking Back My Life.* New York: Summit.

Index

"accidents of private history," 24–26
acting out the trauma, 97
The Alchemy of Race and Rights
(Williams), 6
American Psychiatric Association, 15,
79
Améry, Jean (Hans Maier), 46, 47,
50, 65
anger response: Ilongot headhunting
and bereavement, 27; incompatibility of fear of assailant and,
14; rape survivors and, 13–14, 63,
74–75, 142n.18; research on self-
defense students and, 142n.23. *See
also* emotions

Anglo-American analytic tradition,
24
Aristotle, 13
article 64 (French criminal code),
8
Auschwitz, 47, 48, 52. *See also* Holocaust survivors
Auschwitz and After (Delbo),
73
Austin, J. L., 71, 72
autonomous agency of self, 59–64
autonomy: interactions essential to,
61–62. *See also* control
avocat général (attorney general), 86,
97

tim, 10–11; first-person narratives as basis for, 26; gained by survivor for self, 73; required by listener, 58–59, 62, 72–73; traveling Levite story on lack of, 55–56

Estrich, Susan, 27

experience: feminist philosophy context of personal, 28; gap between memories and, 30–31; personal identification with, 62–63; rape trauma and loss, 20–21, 59–60, 73–74; rape victim's story as access to, 24–26; self as set of ongoing narrative of, 49; social construction/context of, 32–34; traumatic event as "missed," 32

Fackenheim, Emil, 64

La Famiglia (film), 62

female body: used as men's language, 56–57; philosophical rejection of, 42; rape victim's changed awareness of, 46; trauma and relationship with one's own, 44–45, 48–49. *See also* body; women

The Female Fear (Gordon and Riger), 18

feminist ethics, 25

feminist philosophy: first-person narratives in, 24–25, 28–29; interdisciplinary approaches to personal identity by, 39; personal experience context of, 28

feminist theory: on desire for connection/fear of alienation tension, 61; on rape as violence, 93; on relational self, 38, 133n.6, 135n.15, 136n.31

fight or flight response, 40

first-person narratives: bearing witness through, 59, 102–3; cultural repression and rejection of, 57–59; in feminist philosophy, 24–25, 28–29; gender and other biases

exposed by, 26–29; hazard of competing narratives, 34, 94; hazard of perpetuating stereotypes by, 35, 95–96, 144n.7; hazard of presuming to speak for group in, 29–30, 94; hazard of selective memory in, 30–33, 94; importance of listening to, 5–6; involuntary traumatic memories vs., 71–72, 145n.5; obstacle of despair to constructing, 51–52; psychological pressures inhibiting listening to, 57–59; reasons for necessity of, 26, 104, 109–12; recovery through constructing/retelling of, 53–54, 68; regaining control over body through, 54–57. *See also* narrative; rape victim's stories; trauma testimonies

"fractured speech" bouts, 114

Freud, Sigmund, 68, 70, 139n.5

Frug, Mary Joe, 15

Fussell, Paul, 50–51

Gaulin, Ann, 20

God, 11, 24

Gordon, Margaret, 18

"Grief and a Headhunter's Rage" (Rosaldo), 27

Gulf War, 15, 18, 98

Guri, Chaim, 59

Hacking, Ian, 79

Halbwachs, Maurice, 31

Harbour, Kimberly Rae, 15

Harris, Joseph, 120

Harrison, Ross, 4, 5, 6, 7

hate crime, 13

hate speech, 5, 135n.22

Held, Virginia, 24, 28, 61

helplessness, 89–90, 141n.13

Herman, Judith, 40, 47, 110–11

Hirsch, Marianne, 55, 86

narrative: defining, 102; obstacles to reconstructing self, 49–59; remembering through, 59, 72, 97–99, 102–3; the self as, 49, 135n.14. *See also* first-person narratives; rape victim's stories

narrative memories, 30–33

Nedelsky, Jennifer, 61

neurotransmitters, 78, 83

New York Times, 17, 78, 93

Nietzsche, Friedrich, 20, 23, 24, 131n.2

"nomadic subjects," 47–48

object status: narrative to recover from, 56–57, 68; trauma victim's reduction to, 46–47, 55, 56–57, 136n.26

Parfit, Derek, 49

"personality-disintegrating" effects, 136n.32

personhood/identity: changes in Holocaust survivors, 38; interdisciplinary approaches to, 39; loss of personal narrative and contaminated, 133n.3; "personality-disintegrating" effects of trauma on, 136n.32; philosophical consideration of real person's, 134n.9; philosophic interest in, 38–39; rational plan of life essential to, 52; traditional philosophical literature on, 62–63. *See also* the self

pharmaceutical treatment, 77, 78–83

Philadelphia rape survivors' support group, 16, 19–20, 63, 94, 114, 115

philosophy: "accidents of private history" role in, 24–26; argumentative strategy used in, 24; embodied self examined by, 41–49; interest in personal identity by,

38–39; lack of literature on rape in discipline of, 132n.5; personal identity according to traditional, 62–63; "self" defined by, 40; transformation of real persons considered in, 134n.9

Pierce-Baker, Charlotte, 103

Plato, 42, 43

political activism, 77

pornography, 91–92

postmemory phenomenon (children of Holocaust survivors), 55, 143n.2

postmemory of rape, 87–88, 143n.4

"poverty of language," 52

prememory of rape, 87–88

"Pretty Polly" (folk song), 92

The Problems of Philosophy (Russell), 23, 24

Proust, Marcel, 45

Prozac, 60, 78

PTSD (post-traumatic stress disorder): criticism of, 80; *DSM IV* description of, 130n.10; impact of background/circumstances on, 30; pharmaceutical treatment for, 77, 78–83; stigma associated with, 82–83; suffered by rape victims, 15–16; symptoms of, 39–40, 44, 59–60, 80–82. *See also* trauma/traumatic events

rage. *See* anger response

Ranson, Linda Ramzy, 14

"Rape: A Case Study in Political Philosophy" (Harrison), 4–5

rape: denial reaction to, 9; expression as part of recovery, 15–16; FBI estimates on frequency of, 3–4, 129n.2; feminist theory "violence or sex" debate over, 93; as hate crime, 13; helplessness and, 89–90, 141n.13; impact on women by fear of, 18–19; loss experienced

Women's Transit Authority (University of Wisconsin), 17

working through: functions of remembering, 59, 72, 102–3; telling the narrative as part of, 26, 97, 104, 109–12. *See also* recovery

Young, Iris, 14

Zantop, Half, 119–122
Zantop, Susanne, 119–122
Zildzo, Nermina, 48